"simple yet ingenious"

"Simple yet ingenious. . . . I welcome the publication of this book with great enthusiasm. . . . The Teitelbaums have succeeded in communicating what could have been a dauntingly complex subject for the average reader, in a highly readable and understandable fashion."

Portia Iversen
Co-founder, Cure Autism Now
Author, *Strange Son*

"greatly benefits the child"

"This book enables parents to detect signs of autism or other developmental problems in young babies before they start talking. Starting autism therapy at a very early age greatly benefits the child."

Temple Grandin
Author, *Thinking in Pictures*
Emergence: Labeled Autistic

Does Your Baby Have Autism?

Detecting the Earliest Signs of Autism

OSNAT TEITELBAUM
PHILIP TEITELBAUM, PhD

SQUAREONE
PUBLISHERS

The information and advice in this book are based on the research of the authors. Its contents are current and accurate; however, the information presented is not intended to substitute for professional advice. The authors and the publisher urge you to consult with your physician or other qualified health-care provider prior to using any techniques presented within.

Cover Designer: Jeannie Tudor

Illustrations of Children: Cathy Morrison

Cover Photo: Getty Images, Inc.

Editor: Joanne Abrams

Medical Art (pages 15, 16, 43, and 71): Dov Torbin

Typesetter: Gary Rosenberg

Photo Credits: The photo of Leo Kanner on page 5 is used with permission of the Alan Mason Chesney Medical Archives at Johns Hopkins University.
The photo of Hans Asperger on page 5 is used with kind permission of Maria Asperger Felder.
The photo of Temple Grandin on page 8 is used with permission of Joshua Nathaniel Pritikin and William Lawrence Jarrold. Copyright Joshua Nathaniel Pritikin and William Lawrence Jarrold.

Square One Publishers
115 Herricks Road
Garden City Park, NY 11040
(516) 535-2010 • (877) 900-BOOK
www.squareonepublishers.com

Library of Congress Cataloging-in-Publication Data
Teitelbaum, Osnat.
  Does your baby have autism? : detecting the earliest signs of autism / Osnat Teitelbaum, Philip Teitelbaum.
     p. cm.
  Includes bibliographical references and index.
  ISBN 978-0-7570-0240-3 (pbk.)
  1. Autism in children—Diagnosis—Popular works. I. Teitelbaum, Philip. II. Title.

RJ506.A9T428 2008
618.92'85882—dc22
                                2007051346

Printed in the United States of America

10   9   8   7   6   5   4   3   2   1

Contents

*To my teacher, the late Noa Eshkol, who taught me
to see the world in a grain of sand.*

To Bahira and Shelby, who opened the door.

O.T.

*This book is dedicated to the memory of my friend, Dr. Ralph Maurer.
His early work on gait disturbances in autistic children led us to study
the possibility of movement disturbances in autistic-to-be infants.*

P.T.

Acknowledgments

Our work on this book has been spread over many years and was helped by many people. We would like to thank:

The families around the country and in Israel who donated the video footage of their children. They often expressed the hope that by sharing their video material, they might decrease the suffering of others. Without them, this research could not have happened.

Pat Amos, our first supporter, who helped us begin to gather the material that forms the basis of this book.

Portia Iversen and John Shestack of Cure Autism Now (CAN), who financially supported our work when we most needed it.

Danny Homan, who patiently worked with us on our very first draft.

Dr. Joshua B. Fryman, our first computer "mavin," who worked wonders with the primitive electronic equipment available at that time to help us analyze and organize our material.

Joe Kelly, for filling in the void after Joshua went on to graduate school, and especially for designing the websites related to our work.

Jim Qualizza, who continues to help us in all things electronic, digital, and then some.

Dr. Tom Benton, our pediatrician, whose willingness to use the Tilt Test in his clinic promoted its development.

Caroline Niederkohr and her team at the A.C.G. center in Gainesville, Florida (www.acgtherapycenter.com), for their cooperation in connecting us with parents of autistic children.

Andrea Prince, Tana Bleser, and Kathy Berger. Andrea's tireless energy and behind-the-scenes contributions were the oil in the machine that freed us to focus on research. Tana's help in the digital compilation of the images we used went a long way towards bringing this book to print. Kathy joined the team recently and was extremely helpful in doing library research and in the compilation of available treatment centers and therapies.

Helen Horwitz, our partner in Israel, who ran the nursery at Kibbutz Merchavia. Her enthusiasm and insights based on years of working with babies, and her willingness to help, greatly supported our study of typically developing infants.

Uchma and Avner Shafran. Whatever we needed while in Israel (meetings, technical help, and even baby sitting) they were always happily ready to assist us.

Noga Reichman for her unwavering support.

It could only have been divine intervention that led us to our publisher, Rudy Shur. Knowledgeable and attentive to the smallest of details, he cheerfully guided us through the intricacies of the notoriously arduous publishing process. We cannot thank him enough.

One of the perks of working on this book was the opportunity to work with Joanne Abrams, our editor. Nothing escaped her meticulous and fierce intelligence, which made this a better book.

The illustrations showing children's movement patterns are the core of this book. We thank artist Cathy Morrison for so carefully portraying these movements.

Thanks to our son Jonathan, now a junior at Stanford, for so generously dedicating his winter break to reading over our manuscript. Explaining our work in everyday terms was not an easy task, and it couldn't have been done without his keen ear and skill with language.

Finally, we would like to acknowledge the mothers and fathers of autistic children everywhere. In the majority of cases, they are the ones who shoulder the physical burden of the child's day-to-day care. Their daily struggle to create a friendlier world for the autistic child is nothing short of heroic. In this book, we have attempted to give them a simple, practical tool to use and consult in the very first stages of the baby's motor development. We believe that in the world of autism today, nothing is more urgent than the need to drastically lower the age of diagnosis.

*F*oreword

In the early months after our first child's birth, we were already worried that something was wrong. It was not anything specific or anything that we could find in the baby books we'd bought in joyful anticipation of our child's arrival. Our pediatrician could see that something was not quite right, but he could not detect what the problem was any better than we could.

When our son Dov was twenty-one months old, he was diagnosed with autism. By then, speech was not emerging and social interaction was rapidly being displaced by an alarming fascination with patterns of light, objects, and repetitive motion. Now, looking back at early videos of Dov, it is clear that a set of highly identifiable symptoms were present as early as six month of age. It is these symptoms, still unrecognized by parents and physicians, that are the subject of this very important book.

My husband, Jon Shestack, and I started the Cure Autism Now foundation when our son Dov was three, and it was soon after, in 1998, that I read Osnat and Philip Teitelbaum's first paper describing movement disorders in individuals with autism. I was very excited by their work because they were measuring something that was objective and quantifiable, unlike the highly subjective indices of social behavior that had historically been used to define autism. In 1999, I invited Philip and Osnat to give the keynote presentation at the annual Cure Autism Now meeting. To this day, I still run into researchers who attended that presentation, and they say it was an experience they will never forget. The Teitelbaums' special guests were six-year-old twin brothers who at the age of three had been diagnosed with autism at Stanford University. Both brothers had received intensive early intervention, but by the age of six, one was indistinguishable from typically developing children while the other was severely autistic. After presenting his research, which included the early movement differences described in this book, Philip Teitelbaum asked us to view a home video of the twins at age one and, using his criteria, try to determine which of the two children would later become autistic. Once we knew what to look for, it was obvious. One of the twins showed all the early motor signs that Teitelbaum described, while the other did not.

The Teitelbaums' premise was simple yet ingenious: If abnormal motor behavior is observable in children and adults with autism, then these signs were likely to be detectable at a much earlier stage of development. This meant that very early diagnosis could be possible. It also meant that although autism manifested as a social and communication disorder, its underlying cause might not be. This latter implication was important because despite a tremendous increase in autism research over the past decade, the field has continued to be dominated by the behavioral model that was established seventy years ago when autism was first described by Kanner. And despite the enormous advances in technology, molecular biology, and our understanding of the brain in the past decade, autism continues to be diagnosed and described through subjective behavioral observation using criteria that is based on assumptions about the cause and meaning of specific behaviors.

It has been nine years since the Teitelbaums' first paper appeared, and it has been frankly frustrating that this important work has not been more widely disseminated, that it has not been adopted for clinical diagnosis, that it has not been replicated by other labs, and that it has not yet impacted our research paradigm or been used to accelerate the race to connect phenotype to genotype in autism. It is for all these reasons that I welcome the publication of this book with great enthusiasm. When I asked why he thought there has not been more followup of his work in the field, Philip Teiltelbaum explained it this way: "It is not so much that science is slow, but in this case, the major reason is that the other scientists in the field of Autism do not have the EWMN method (the Eshkol Wachman Movement Notation is a system of movement analysis that was created in 1958 by Prof. Emeritus Noa Eshkol of Tel Aviv University and her then-student, Prof. Emeritus Avraham Wachman, see: http://www.movementnotation.com/ and http://biology.mcgill.ca/perspage/ew_page.htm for more information). An analogy can be found in the work of Louis Pasteur. Because he used a microscope, he could see germs where others could not. In addition, it should be realized that as in all other fields (music, mathematics, computer, software, etc.) a suitable language is a must in order to start gathering information and to formulate the concepts which integrate it."

In their book, the Teitelbaums have succeeded in communicating what could have been a dauntingly complex subject for the average reader, in a highly readable and understandable fashion. The very early signs of possible autism are broken down into three main categories: movement, symmetry, and motor development, and each is described in an accessible, common sense manner. The authors encourage and empower parents to be proactive in the investigation of suspected developmental problems in their own child. Typically parents are told to turn these matters over to a professional even though, as the Teitelbaums so accurately state, no one knows a child better than his or her parent. Even today it is still considered a radical statement to proclaim, as the authors do: "You don't have to be an expert in child development to identify autism-related behavior."

The Teitelbaums' research is a welcome paradigm shift in the way we observe, describe, diagnose, and even define autism. But perhaps most important of all is that these very early warning signs can alert parents and physicians to the possibility of development gone astray so that therapeutic interventions may begin as early as possible.

It is my hope that this book will hasten a departure from the old behavioral model that has dominated the autism field since its beginnings, and that it will inspire further expansion and replication of the Teitelbaums' important work. I join Philip and Osnat in affirming that parents are the greatest experts when it comes to their own child and in encouraging parents to have confidence in their own observations. I am privileged to know Philip and Osnat and their amazing work, and I am grateful for their unflagging dedication to helping our children.

Portia Iversen
Co-founder, Cure Autism Now
Author, *Strange Son*

A Word About Gender

Your child is certainly as likely to be a boy as a girl. However, our language does not provide us with a genderless pronoun. To avoid using the awkward "he/she" or the impersonal "it" when referring to a child, while still giving equal time to both sexes, the feminine pronouns "she," "her," and "hers" have been used in odd-numbered chapters, while the male "he," "him," and "his" appear in all the rest. This decision was made in the interest of simplicity and clarity.

Preface

Our observations of movement patterns in infants who were later diagnosed as autistic started after Philip attended a lecture given by our good friend, the late Dr. Ralph Maurer. A pioneer in autism research, Dr. Maurer showed videos of autistic children between the ages of three and eleven, and compared their atypical gaits—their walking patterns—to those of Parkinson's patients. The videos showed marked similarities between the young children and the elderly people with Parkinson's.

Philip was intrigued. He reasoned that if autistic children exhibit atypical movements when they are three years old, they probably exhibit unusual movement patterns in infancy, before traditional methods can diagnose them as being autistic. To learn if this idea was correct, we needed to find children who had already been diagnosed with autism, and view videotapes made of them when they were still infants. Who would have videotapes of this type? The children's parents.

We placed ads in the newsletters of local organizations formed to help parents with autistic children. Soon, parents started sending in videotapes, and Osnat began watching them and recording their movements. To do so, she used a very special system of analysis called Eshkol-Wachman Movement Notation (EWMN). First published in 1958 by Noa Eshkol and Avraham Wachman, EWMN is a movement language. Using it, one can observe movement patterns, write them down, and read them. By doing so, it is possible to find order in seemingly chaotic and meaningless patterns of movement. It's worth noting that without EWMN, the movements of these infants could not have been meaningfully compared with those of nonautistic infants. As a rule, a verbal language such as English is simply not intended to adequately describe movement. For instance, if someone tells you to lift your hand above your head, you could interpret this instruction in a variety of ways. You might first lift your arm forward and then raise your hand upwards. Or you might lift your arm out to the side and move it in an arc until your hand was over your head. With EWMN, the movement can be described and written down in a way that leaves no room for misinterpretation.

Because of the technology of the time, watching and recording movements was a slow process. The tapes were usually made of birthdays, holidays, vacations—special events in the family's life. It took time to locate uninterrupted sequences of the infants' movements and record the path of each limb separately so that we could form a lasting "image" in symbols. We could not freeze images or replay key sections at different speeds. Instead, Osnat had to run each tape over and over again. To focus on the movement, she turned the sound off, thus eliminating social context. It took five years to finish the initial study of the children's movements.

As Osnat watched the children turn over, sit up, stand, and walk, certain atypical movement patterns began to repeat themselves. It soon became clear that even in the first months of life—long before these children exhibited the language and socialization problems normally used to diagnose autism—there were signs that something was wrong. Most children later diagnosed as being autistic either had trouble learning first-year motor skills such as righting and sitting, or were unable to master these skills at all.

Each time Osnat noticed an atypical movement pattern, she discussed it with Philip, who drew on his background in neurology to better understand the motion. This process, too, was not easy. Sitting or lying on our office floor, we would often try to duplicate the movements we saw so that we could better comprehend what was happening to these children.

Our original 1998 paper, "Movement Analysis in Infancy May Be Useful for Early Diagnosis of Autism," published in *Proceedings of the National Academy of Sciences (PNAS)*, was based on our observation of seventeen children. Not long after the journal article appeared, *The New York Times* published an article on our findings, and we began receiving a flood of videotapes from parents of both autistic and Asperger's kids. Like the earlier videotapes, the new ones showed certain atypical movements over and over again. To date, we have found these movements in well over a hundred tapes.

Often, the videotapes we received were accompanied by letters from the children's parents. We were struck by the fact that many parents had *known* that something was wrong with their infants early on, but were unable to convince the child's physician that there was a problem. The letter on page xv is typical of many we received.

In addition to receiving videotapes and letters from moms and dads all over the country, we often were approached by parents at scientific

Dear Dr. Teitelbaum,

I have read with great interest your 1998 paper entitled "Movement Analysis in Infancy May Be Useful for Early Diagnosis of Autism." I have a sixteen-year-old autistic son and now have an eight-month-old granddaughter who I believe may be showing early signs of autism. She also has many signs of a movement disorder. At 8 mos. old, she has never turned over either way, and in fact hates being on her belly, shows no idea of how to crawl and sit, but needs support if on the floor alone. She does many of the things you explained in your paper, and when I use the tilt test, she does not straighten her head. The problem is even many of the best doctors around here tell us it is too early to diagnose autism, and they even recommend a wait and see attitude for her movement problems that seem to me to be quite severe.

I wonder if you would know anyone in this area of the country who would take our concerns seriously and see us? I am not looking for a diagnosis, but help in intervening in what might be a case of autism if things aren't worked on now and if my granddaughter isn't helped to optimal functioning. We have been working on gaining her attention on a more regular basis and helping her to be more responsive to us, but we don't know what to do about her movement difficulties. Do you have any other suggestions?

None of the doctors I know who are the main ones around here to diagnose autism, profess to know that a movement disorder can be present early on. Is this not common knowledge in the diagnostic literature?

Thank you for any help you can give me.

Sincerely,

M.G.

conferences. After we reported the early infant behavior of children later diagnosed with autism or Asperger's, parents would say, "You just described my child." It soon became clear that many parents needed help. They needed to know about the specific movements they should look for to determine if their infants might be at risk for autism or Asperger's. They also needed child-care professionals to be aware that not every child "outgrows" motor skill problems, and that certain atypical movements, when they persist over time, may indicate the neurological damage associated with autism.

The autism community is large and full of competing and often contradictory information. The one thing that autism professionals seem to agree on is this: The earlier autism is diagnosed and therapy is begun, the greater the chance that the child can be helped. It is our hope that this book will open the door to a new approach to autism diagnosis, allowing parents and professionals alike to help children early in life, when this assistance may be of greatest value.

*"Know rather that we must turn to nature itself,
to the observation of the body in health and disease,
to learn the truth."*

—HIPPOCRATES

*I*ntroduction

In the early 1940s, physicians Leo Kanner and Hans Asperger published studies of children who showed, in Kanner's words, "autistic aloneness." These children had a preference for objects over people, and seemed to tune out everyone around them. They also exhibited language difficulties as well as problems in nonverbal communication. Soon, children who shared these traits were described as having *autism*.

Now, many decades after these physicians performed their work, the diagnosis of autism still relies heavily on the criteria provided by Kanner and Asperger. Most experts diagnose autism largely by evaluating social interaction, language acquisition, and nonverbal communication. While this may be an effective means of determining if a child is autistic, it presents a problem: Social interaction and communication skills are usually not apparent until a child is two years of age, and perhaps even older. Yet experts agree that the sooner intervention is provided, the better the outcome for the child. We now know that autism is a sign of neurological impairment—damage to the brain. During a child's first year, the brain is developing rapidly and is better able to compensate for areas that are not maturing properly. While experience shows that appropriate therapy can help even older autistic children overcome many of their problems, therapy could be so much more effective if it were begun earlier in life.

For almost two decades, our research has shown us a way to identify the signs of autism without relying on socialization or language skills. By observing the atypical movement patterns of babies and using our combined specialties—movement analysis and neuroscience—to understand these behaviors, we have learned that some potential signs of autism and Asperger's syndrome can be seen as early as the first few months of life. This book was designed to share our findings with you.

Does Your Baby Have Autism? is the first book to provide a means of identifying precursors of autism during a child's first year—before he acquires language and begins to interact with others. By viewing videotapes of infants who were later diagnosed as having autism or Asperger's syndrome, and comparing them with videotapes of nonautistic children of the same age, we have been able to identify motor skill problems that may indicate the neurological impairment associated with these disorders. During the first year of life, the typical infant learns to right himself, crawl, sit up, and walk, and each of these milestones is achieved through specific movements. This gives us benchmarks against which we can evaluate the motor development of autistic-to-be kids. What we have found is that autistic children show movements that are very different from those of typical kids. In the past, many parents of autistic children seem to have known "intuitively" that there was something wrong with their infant—only to be told to wait until the signs of autism were more evident, and could be identified by professionals. But now you don't have to be an expert in child development to identify autism-related behavior. With the help of this book, any parent, grandparent, or other caregiver can easily spot the telltale movements that indicate a potential neurological problem.

Does Your Baby Have Autism? begins by providing a concise history of autism, defining the disorder, and examining how the modern medical community diagnoses and treats autism and Asperger's syndrome. We then introduce you to our research, and most important, to our revolutionary way of detecting movements that can signal the development of these conditions.

Chapter 2 explores symmetry and explains how your understanding of this concept can help you identify children who may later develop autism. Human beings are symmetrical not only in their physical makeup, but also in the way they move. This is important because it makes it easy to see the asymmetrical movements that can indicate neurological problems such as autism.

Reflexes are the subject of Chapter 3. This chapter will first fill you in on the reflexes that are present from birth, and then look at some reflexes that are acquired during the first year of life. You will learn that in a typical infant, these reflexes appear and fade at predictable times. When they don't act as expected, they interfere with motor development, providing another means of identifying children who may have autism.

Chapter 4 introduces the Ladder of Motor Development—the transitional process that a baby experiences as he moves from relative helplessness to the independence enjoyed when he masters walking. Again, the average baby's movement up the ladder is fairly predictable. But the progress of a child with autism generally does not conform to that of the nonautistic child.

Chapters 5, 6, 7, and 8 each examine an important rung on the Ladder of Motor Development. Chapter 5 focuses on righting (rolling over); Chapter 6, on crawling; Chapter 7, on sitting; and Chapter 8, on walking—the zenith of the ladder. In each chapter, you will first learn how this motor milestone is reached by the typical infant. You will then see the problems encountered by children who were later diagnosed with autism or Asperger's syndrome. Throughout each chapter, illustrations will help you understand exactly what you should be looking for. Just as important, a What You Can Do section will first guide you in effectively observing and recording your child's progress, and then provide exercises and activities that can promote your infant's motor development.

Chapter 9, "Seeking Help," assists you in doing just that. The chapter begins with tips on effectively explaining your child's motor problems to your infant's doctor. It then introduces you to several programs that can provide your infant with the help he needs. Finally, it discusses the option of putting together a team of specialists, therapies, and activities that are specifically geared for your child.

We know that because you are so close to your baby and care for him on a daily basis, you are the person most likely to first observe problems in your infant's behavior. For that reason, we have included in this book many of the tools you'll need to assist your child. An Observation Journal, which begins on page 131, offers a place for you to record your child's movements, helping you create a clear picture of his development. A Suggested Reading List (page 125) gives you an opportunity to learn more about autism and Asperger's syndrome, and a Resources section (page 117) guides you in finding appropriate programs and therapists.

One of our goals in writing this book has been to foster communication between you and your child's physician. We believe that once you are able to pinpoint atypical movement patterns and show them to your doctor, he will be more willing and better able to help you. Many parents feel that something may be amiss with their child, but are unable to convey the problem to their child's doctor. This book is intended to fill the gap between parent and physician.

Body movements are an external mirror of the workings of the nervous system. Once you learn about the specific motions associated with autism, we believe you can identify at-risk infants when they are only six to eight months of age. This doesn't mean that your baby won't require help in climbing the Ladder of Motor Development. It does mean that your child will be able to get the assistance he needs at a time when it is easiest for him to learn, grow, and move toward a more fulfilling future.

Before you turn the page and start learning more about autism, we want to make one more important point. If others insist that your child's problems will work out in time, but you feel that he needs help *now,* you must act on your beliefs. Remember that you are your child's first and best advocate. Stick to your guns.

CHAPTER 1

What Is Autism?

Autism is not a new condition. Indeed, the word "autism" was coined more than a century ago. Over the years, however, our definition of autism has changed, as has our understanding of this condition.

This chapter first provides a concise history of autism and attempts to describe this disorder. It then looks at how the medical community currently defines, diagnoses, and treats autism. Finally, we briefly introduce you to our own research on this disorder—research that, we believe, offers new hope to infants everywhere.

A BRIEF HISTORY OF AUTISM

Prior to the 1900s, autism as a diagnosis was nonexistent. Those people who had what is now called autism were diagnosed with another disorder—usually, Juvenile Schizophrenia or mental retardation. For this reason, autistic children were often institutionalized.

Leo Kanner

Eugen Bleuler, a Swiss psychiatrist, first introduced the term *autism* in 1911, basing the word on the Greek *autos,* meaning "self." Yet Bleuler did not use the term to describe people that we would now identify as autistic, but applied it to people with schizophrenia who showed an extreme withdrawal from social life.

Several decades after Bleuler's coining of the term, autism was given a new meaning. In the late 1930s, an Austrian-born psychiatrist named Leo Kanner began conducting a case study of eleven children at the Johns Hopkins Hospital in Baltimore, Maryland. This culminated in Kanner's classic 1943 publication "Autistic Disturbances of Affective Contact," in which he described the children in his study as having "extreme autistic aloneness." A year later, Hans Asperger, an Austrian pediatrician working independently of Kanner, published "Autistic Psychopathy in Childhood." In his article, Asperger described several children who, although

Hans Asperger

The works of Leo
Kanner and Hans
Asperger formed the
basis of the modern
study of autism.

they differed in some respects from the patients observed by Kanner, shared the trait of seeming remote and uninterested in other people.

Despite the fact that neither Kanner nor Asperger had access to today's medical technology, their observations are fundamental to the field of autism today. Both doctors believed that the children they studied suffered from an underlying disturbance. Most interesting were the features of autistic behavior described by the two doctors. They included:

- **"Autistic aloneness," meaning a tendency to fixate on one stereotypic (repetitive) activity, shutting out anything, whether a person or a situation, from the outside world.** This separation of self from the rest of the world is the cornerstone of what is referred to as autism. In fact, at the time that Kanner and Asperger were writing, many autistic children were at first considered deaf because they seemed completely oblivious to the sounds around them.

- **A preference of things over people.** Autistic children ignore and avoid the people around them, including their parents. In fact, they appear to regard people as "things" that are to be either disregarded or dealt with, without any emotional attachment.

- **Language difficulties, which can take a variety of forms.** Some children with autism do not speak as early as typical children do. Some don't speak until three years of age; a few, not until their late teens. Some children start to "babble" on time, and then regress to a form of speech called *echolalia,* in which they repeat all or part of what was just said to them. Many never use the first-person pronoun "I," but instead, refer to themselves as "you." For instance, an autistic child might state *"You* want candy," when she actually means *"I* want candy." More often than not, it is language difficulties that first draw attention to a child with autism.

- **Ritualistic and obsessive behavior, which can take a variety of forms.** Once an action is carried out in one way, an autistic child will often insist that it always be performed in that manner. In other words, these children insist on "sameness." For instance, when traveling from point A to point B, a child may insist on always taking the route used the first time she went from A to B. Even the smallest of changes in routine can lead to a temper tantrum. Autistic children may also have special systems of arranging favorite objects.

- **An intolerance of loud noises, some movements, and other specific sensory stimuli.** Autistic children have been known to fear elevators, vacuum cleaners, mechanical toys, running water, and even the wind, and to go into a panic when these things are present. Kanner, who was the first to note this phenomenon, felt that the problem was caused not by the noise or movement itself, but by its intrusion into the child's aloneness. Since then, other interpretations have been offered. (See the inset on page 8.)

- **Remarkable feats of memory and other unusual mental abilities.** Although this is not true of every autistic child, some children with this diagnosis have an amazing memory for specific things, such as poems or sports trivia; are able to perform mathematical computations that border on genius; have astounding musical abilities; or exhibit other extraordinary talents.

- **Lack of smiling during and sometimes beyond infancy, as well as lack of facial expression when speaking.** Kanner first reported that many autistic children do not smile, and that their speech is often not accompanied by facial expressions or gestures. Our own observations have shown that some children later diagnosed as autistic did not smile at all as infants. This is sometimes due to a form of paralysis called Moebius mouth, which is discussed on page 20.

It is important to note that both Kanner and Asperger commented on a possible relationship between autism and schizophrenia, but agreed that they are separate conditions. The most significant difference between the two disorders is that even the earliest onset of schizophrenia is preceded by at least two years of average development, while autistic children show evidence of their condition from the very beginning of life. This is why, as we will explain in later chapters, it is possible to detect autism fairly early in infancy.

Perhaps because of World War II, at first, little response was generated by Kanner and Asperger's findings. But during the seventies and eighties, a number of people—Lorna Wing, Michael Rutter, William Condon, Uta Frith, and Edward Ornitz, to name just a few—further explored the nature of autism, searched for its causes, and devised methods of treatment. By the time of Leo Kanner's death in 1981, his findings, as well as those of fellow pioneer Hans Asperger, had worldwide acknowledgment, and autism was recognized as a valid diagnosis.

Interest in autism has continued, and many studies have focused on the disorder, with strides being made in identifying its cause. It should be noted that back in the 1940s, Leo Kanner's observations of autistic chil-

Although autism pioneers Leo Kanner and Hans Asperger originally explored a potential relationship between autism and schizophrenia, the two scientists ultimately agreed that they are two separate conditions.

A Personal Perspective on Autism

Leo Kanner may have been the first person to write about the autistic child's intolerance of loud noises and unexpected movements. (See the discussion on page 6.) But Kanner was certainly not the last to remark on this phenomenon, because an aversion to certain sensory stimulation is characteristic of many autistic people.

A number of experts, including Kanner, have tried to explain the autistic child's sometimes exaggerated reaction to stimuli that would seem insignificant or even pleasant to the nonautistic child. A most intriguing and revealing account is that offered by Temple Grandin, a high-functioning autistic woman who now enjoys a successful career designing equipment for livestock and teaching animal science at Colorado State University. In her autobiography, *Emergence: Labeled Autistic,* Grandin presents a fascinating picture of how the autistic person experiences the world around her.

From the time she was a child, Temple Grandin was overly sensitive to noise and touch. Grandin describes her hearing as being akin to wearing a hearing aid that is always set on "super loud." Even though Grandin always yearned for a mother's embrace, a hug was experienced as a frightening "tidal wave" of stimulation, while any unfamiliar clothes felt unbearably scratchy

Temple Grandin

and itchy. Her response to loud noise was to simply tune out all sound, causing her to sometimes seem deaf. When faced with hugs or other unwanted tactile stimulation, she would flinch and turn away.

Temple Grandin's autism did not disappear. She still has the brain abnormalities that most likely caused her autism. She is still annoyed by high-pitched noises and dislikes places like crowded malls and airports, which provide many confusing and competing sounds. And she still suffers from oversensitivity to touch. But Grandin has come a long way since her difficult childhood, and is now able to better cope with irritating stimuli. In books, lectures, and articles about her condition, she credits her progress to excellent speech therapy; a mother who personally schooled her in reading; an imaginative teacher who steered her toward an appropriate career; and antidepressants, which have controlled her anxiety and enhanced her speech and sociability. Because of her experiences, both positive and negative, she emphasizes the need for a variety of programs that are individualized for each child. Most of all, she stresses that early, intense intervention provides the best prognosis for autistic children.

dren and their families led to the "refrigerator mother" school of thought. Popularized by child psychologist Bruno Bettelheim, the refrigerator mother label was based on the notion that autism is caused by the mother's lack of emotional warmth. This idea was eventually discredited, and other explanations of the disorder have since been offered. Some people have suggested that thimerosal, a mercury-based preservative used in routine childhood vaccines, plays a part in the development of autism. This is a highly controversial issue. There is, however, strong evidence that DNA variants—genetics, in other words—lie at the roots of autism. This would explain why in some families, as many as three or four children have been diagnosed with the condition. Examination of the brains of autistic individuals has revealed abnormalities within the brain stem and cerebellum. (See page 42 for information on the anatomy of the brain.) The mechanism through which the genes can cause atypical brain development is not yet known.

During the first half of the twentieth century, some researchers believed that autism was caused by a lack of parental warmth. This idea was discredited later in the century.

AUTISM NOW

Autism is now considered one of several conditions that fall under the umbrella term *Autism Spectrum Disorders* (ASD). Opinions differ as to exactly which conditions are covered by this term. Other than autism, many experts include Asperger's syndrome, Childhood Disintegrative Disorder, Rett syndrome, and Pervasive Developmental Disorder—Not Otherwise Specified. All five ASD conditions are characterized by impaired social interactions and communication skills, as well as repetitive patterns of behavior. The inset on page 10 presents the criteria used to diagnose autistic disorders as they appear in the American Psychiatric Association's publication *Diagnostic and Statistical Manual of Mental Disorders.*

Of the five ASD conditions, autism and Asperger's syndrome are the most common, and it is these two disorders that we explore in this book. What is the difference between autism and Asperger's? Autism is usually defined as a developmental disorder characterized by problems with social interaction, language and other communication, and learning. It can also involve repetitive behavior, the desire for routine, and remarkable mental abilities. People with Asperger's syndrome have many of the same characteristics, but tend to have higher IQs and develop language at a normal age. Yet they often lack the ability to recognize social cues and respond appropriately to social situations. Moreover, people with Asperger's often develop specialized interests and talk about them

Diagnostic Criteria for Autistic Disorder

The *Diagnostic and Statistical Manual of Mental Disorders (DSM)* is a handbook designed for mental health professionals. Published by the American Psychiatric Association, it is used worldwide by clinicians and researchers. Following are the *DSM's* most recent criteria for diagnosing autism, Asperger's syndrome, and other Autism Spectrum Disorders.

A. A total of six (or more) items from (1), (2), and (3), with at least two from (1), and one each from (2) and (3):

(1) *qualitative impairment in social interaction, as manifested by at least two of the following:*

(a) *marked impairment in the use of multiple nonverbal behaviors such as eye-to-eye gaze, facial expression, body postures, and gestures to regulate social interaction*

(b) *failure to develop peer relationships appropriate to developmental level*

(c) *a lack of spontaneous seeking to share enjoyment, interests, or achievements with other people (e.g., by a lack of showing, bringing, or pointing out objects of interest)*

(d) *lack of social or emotional reciprocity*

(2) *qualitative impairments in communication as manifested by at least one of the following:*

(a) *delay in, or total lack of, the development of spoken language (not accompanied by an attempt to compensate through alternative modes of communication such as gesture or mime)*

(b) *in individuals with adequate speech, marked impairment in the ability to initiate or sustain a conversation with others*

(c) *stereotyped and repetitive use of language or idiosyncratic language*

(d) *lack of varied, spontaneous make-believe play or social imitative play appropriate to developmental level*

(3) *restricted repetitive and stereotyped patterns of behavior, interests, and activities, as manifested by at least one of the following:*

(a) *encompassing preoccupation with one or more stereotyped and restricted patterns of interest that is abnormal either in intensity or focus*

(b) *apparently inflexible adherence to specific, nonfunctional routines or rituals*

(c) *stereotyped and repetitive motor mannerisms (e.g., hand or finger flapping or twisting, or complex whole-body movements)*

(d) *persistent preoccupation with parts of objects*

B. *Delays or abnormal functioning in at least one of the following areas, with onset prior to age 3 years: (1) social interaction, (2) language as used in social communication, or (3) symbolic or imaginative play.*

C. *The disturbance is not better accounted for by Rett's Disorder or Childhood Disintegrative Disorder.*

obsessively using adult language. This is why Asperger's is sometimes referred to as *Little Professor Syndrome.* Some experts have also observed that Asperger's children are clumsy in their movements, and this clumsiness is used by some as a specific marker for Asperger's syndrome. It should be noted, though, that people diagnosed with autism can be clumsy as well.

In this book, we use the words "autistic" and "autism" as umbrella terms to refer to both autism and Asperger's syndrome. The term "Asperger's" is used to refer to only that specific syndrome.

WHAT TREATMENTS ARE OFFERED FOR AUTISM?

Researchers now agree that autistic behavior indicates some type of neurological impairment. But because the exact nature of this impairment and the severity and presentation of symptoms vary so much from individual to individual, no one specific treatment exists. Instead, a variety of therapies are available. These include but are not limited to the following. (To learn more about the treatments listed below as well as other therapies, see Chapter 9.)

Although many of the disorder's traits appear psychological in nature, autism is now known to be a neurological condition.

- **Applied Behavior Analysis (ABA).** Based on the work of B.F. Skinner, this method uses positive reinforcement to shape appropriate behavior and promote learning in autistic children. It involves one-on-one interaction between a child and an ABA professional for as many as forty hours a week.

- **Facilitated Communication.** Designed to allow communication by individuals without functional speech, this method involves a facilitator who uses physical contact to help the disabled person express her thoughts through a keyboard, picture board, or speech synthesizer.

- **Floortime.** Developed by Dr. Stanley Greenspan, Floortime is intensive one-on-one therapy in which a child and an adult—either a trained therapist or a parent—engage in imitation play intended to help the child master developmental milestones.

- **Medication therapy.** Medication therapy uses drugs to treat autism's various symptoms, such as hyperactivity, anxiety, and aggressive behavior.

- **Nutritional therapy.** This approach uses supplements and/or a special diet free of gluten (wheat) and casein (dairy) to treat the autistic child.

- **Occupational therapy.** Through the use of real-life activities, occupational therapy develops the practical skills needed for daily living, as well as play and social skills.

- **Physical therapy.** This therapy uses exercises and physical activities to teach motor skills such as walking and running, and to improve general posture, balance, coordination, and strength.

- **Sensory integration therapy.** Based on the work of A. Jean Ayres, this therapy teaches the nervous system to properly interpret sensory input—the five senses, as well as the senses of movement and body position—and respond in an appropriate manner. The result is enhanced concentration, motor skills, and behavior.

- **Speech and language therapy.** This therapy is designed to improve both verbal and nonverbal communication skills.

- **The Tomatis Method.** Based on the work of Dr. Alfred A. Tomatis, the Tomatis Method provides the child with specialized auditory stimuli of different frequencies. The purpose is to decrease hypersensitivity to sound, enhance language and social skills, and otherwise lessen the symptoms associated with autism.

Because every child with autism is unique, with her own strengths and weaknesses, parents often experiment with different therapies, and combine these treatments with recreational activities that can further build skills.

Because it is so difficult to match each child with an appropriate treatment, parents often experiment with multiple therapies at the same time in an effort to deal with their child's various problems. Many concerned parents also enroll their children in vision therapy, music therapy, horseback riding, yoga, and other activities to help them develop weaker skills.

HOW SUCCESSFUL ARE CURRENT TREATMENTS OF AUTISM?

Since autism and Asperger's were first recognized in the 1940s, the search for truly effective treatment has been frustrating to both parents and professionals. While many children have been helped, many others have not.

Let's look at Applied Behavior Analysis, mentioned on page 11. ABA is widely accepted by both parents and doctors largely because it has been highly researched, and because its effectiveness is supported by numerous anecdotal stories. One study published in 1987 stated that by the age of seven, about half of the forty test children undergoing this therapy were able to join mainstream classes, showing an impressive rate of success in comparison with the untreated group. Still, half of the children undergoing ABA were *not* able to perform like nonautistic children of the same age.

Other statistics support the limited effectiveness of current treatments. For instance, researchers say that with therapy, 25 percent of autistic children are able to score in a normal IQ range and to function in public school. Yet 25 percent of those treated never develop language skills.

The above statistics are not being cited to denigrate the many dedicated professionals who treat autistic children, or to criticize the valuable therapies they provide. Rather, like many of the experts in the field, we believe that the major problem with current treatments is that they are being started too late in a child's life. In fact, one of the few things the autism community agrees on is the value of early intervention. The nervous system—which is at the center of autism and Asperger's syndrome—is most easily shaped during the first few months of life. At that time, the brain is more "plastic" and better able to compensate for areas that are failing to develop properly. According to Dr. Rebecca Landa, Director of the Center for Autism and Related Disorders at the Kennedy Krieger Institute in Baltimore, Maryland, evidence indicates that if children with autism were diagnosed at a younger age, earlier intervention would ultimately lead to far better outcomes than are currently possible, making a tremendous difference in the lives of children and their families.

Why aren't children usually diagnosed with autism or Asperger's during infancy, when they can be most easily helped? If you look at the definition of autism provided on page 9, as well as the inset on page 10, you'll see that the diagnosis of this disorder focuses on social interaction, on language acquisition, and on learning skills. These are all aspects of development that become most apparent when a child is at least two years of age, rather than when she's an infant. The American Academy of Pediatrics recently stressed the importance of early diagnosis by urging that every child be screened *twice* for autism by age two. But again, they advise pediatricians to look for lack of babbling, no single words by the age of sixteen months, not turning when the parent says the baby's name, and other social and language-related cues—symptoms that are not likely to be helpful during the first year of life. What's needed, then, is a method of detecting this problem as soon after birth as possible.

A NEW WAY TO DIAGNOSE AUTISM

By examining home videos made of infants who were later diagnosed as having autism or Asperger's syndrome, we have found that it is not only possible but actually *easy* to recognize precursors of these disorders in infants who are six to eight months of age, and sometimes even younger. The key to this early recognition is motor skills—movement, in other

Autism professionals agree that earlier intervention would lead to far better outcomes for children with autism.

words. You see, during the first year of life, the typical infant reaches certain motor milestones, learning to right himself (turn from his back to his stomach), crawl, sit up, and walk. Moreover, he accomplishes each of these tasks in specific ways by using specific movements. The child later diagnosed as autistic, however, generally shows very different movements, and often fails to meet motor milestones as expected. This enables the observant parent to detect the potential for autism long before a child is old enough to interact socially or to start speaking. Once a problem in motor development is detected, it can be brought to the attention of a professional, who can provide help for the infant at a time when her brain is better able to change and adjust.

In this chapter, you have learned about autism—its history, its symptoms, and its treatments. Most important, you've discovered the need to diagnose autism as early as possible, when therapy can be most effective. Fortunately, you don't have to be a trained professional to detect the early signs of autism. *Any* parent can learn to identify the early motor skill problems that may signal a disorder. The next chapter will begin your education by introducing you to the concept of symmetry—an early clue to normal infant development.

CHAPTER 2

Symmetry

Symmetry is everywhere in nature. Take a walk outside, and you'll see that both animals and plants have symmetrical body shapes and patterns. If, for instance, you divide a leaf in half, you will discover that one half mirrors the shape of the other—not perfectly, but closely.

We human beings are as symmetrical as the natural world around us, not only in the way we look, but also in the way we move. Why is this important? Symmetry is the norm, so when a child moves in a way that is *asymmetrical*—when one side is more active than the other side, for instance—it signals a problem. And in some cases, that problem is autism. Moreover, this asymmetry can be detected when a baby is only a few weeks old, providing an early warning of developmental delays and possible neurological damage.

This chapter first explores symmetry in a little more detail. It then looks at asymmetry in infants and, most important, it explains how you can easily identify this problem in your own child, and even start taking steps to correct it.

THE IMPORTANCE OF SYMMETRY

Like the rest of our anatomy, the brain is symmetrical in structure. It is made up of two hemispheres, the left brain and the right brain, with a big fold in the center. The left side of the brain controls the right side of the body, and the right side of the brain controls the body's left side. (See Figure 2.1.) Linking the two halves is the *corpus callosum*, a thick bridge of nerve tissue that allows the hemispheres to work together. (See Figure 2.2. For more information on brain anatomy, see page 42.)

When a child moves in a way that is symmetrical, it indicates that both sides of the brain are developing in the same way. When a child moves in

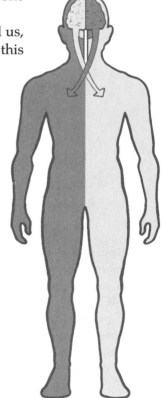

Figure 2.1
The Brain's Control of the Body

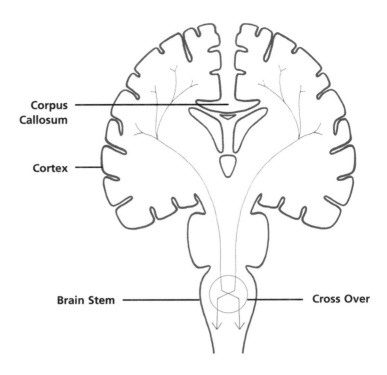

**Figure 2.2
A Cross-Section
of the Brain**

The corpus callosum
connects the
hemispheres of the
brain, allowing them
to work together.

a way that is persistently asymmetrical, however, it most likely shows weakness on one side of the brain. Weakness on the left side of the child's body indicates damage or delay in development of the right side of the brain. Weakness on the right side of his body indicates damage or delay in development of the left side of the brain.

APPRECIATING SYMMETRY

Human beings are
symmetrical both in
form and in function.
As a typical child
develops, the two sides
of his body mature more
or less in the same way
and at the same time.

Although you may have never given it much thought, we are all symmetrical. *Bilateral symmetry*—being composed of two mirror-image halves—is a fundamental organizing principle of our bodies. All of our limbs and most of our organs come in pairs, one on each side. Those features that don't come in pairs, such as the nose and the mouth, tend to be arranged along the imaginary midline that divides the body into two identical halves.

But symmetry is to be found in more than our anatomy. Our motor development is also symmetrical. By this, we mean that even though each baby tends to develop at his own pace—a pace that may differ from that of other babies—his two sides develop more or less in the same way and at the same time. A few examples will make this statement clearer. When

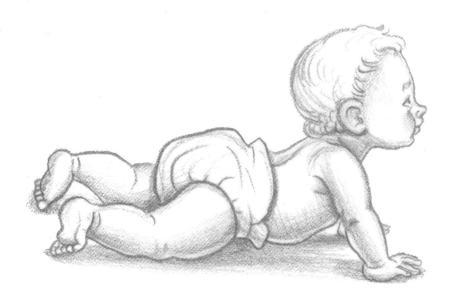

**Figure 2.3
A Three-Month-Old "Peels" His Head From the Floor**

When a baby supports himself with both arms positioned in the same way, it indicates symmetrical development.

a healthy three-month-old infant is placed on his stomach, he "peels" his head and the upper part of this chest from the surface, and supports himself with *both* of his forearms. Moreover, the two forearms are positioned in the same manner—pointing forward and spread about a chest-width apart. (See Figure 2.3.) This enables the infant to support and balance his torso, freeing his head so that he can explore his environment with greater freedom. Similarly, if a healthy infant is lying on his back and someone dangles a toy above him, he can respond equally well with *either* side of his body by reaching for the toy with his left arm or his right arm. This amazing symmetry can be seen even when a baby is only a few weeks old.

Before we further discuss both symmetries and asymmetries, a word should be said about dominance of one side of the body over the other. All adults have a dominant side of the body—one side that we use more than the other. We are either right-handed or left-handed, for instance. Isn't this also true of infants? The fact is that dominance doesn't occur until a child is four or five years old. When a baby is only a few weeks or months old, there should be no overt preference of one side of the body over the other.

Although every adult has a dominant side of the body, children under four or five years of age should not show a preference for using one side of the body over the other.

RECOGNIZING ASYMMETRY

You now know that from the time an infant is born, symmetry is a ruling principle of both his physical and motor development. When he begins

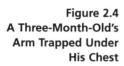

**Figure 2.4
A Three-Month-Old's
Arm Trapped Under
His Chest**

This asymmetrical position deprives the baby of much-needed support.

reaching for objects, ideally, he should be equally capable of reaching for them with either his right hand or his left hand. He should be able to prop himself up with both arms equally well, and to turn his head in either direction. Eventually, he should be able to crawl and, ultimately, walk using both legs with equal proficiency.

How do asymmetries show themselves? Let's go back to the infant who props himself up with his arms, pulling himself up so that he can move his head and look around. If you look at Figure 2.4, you'll see an infant who is lying on his stomach with his left arm trapped under his chest. If it occurs persistently, this asymmetrical position—which is not usually seen in babies—deprives the infant of support by making his left arm inaccessible. The position also causes the baby to lean or fall to his left, forcing him to spend a great deal of energy attempting to keep himself balanced.

An asymmetry in movement that is apparent during the first few months of life may become more pronounced as the child gets older. In other words, an asymmetry that shows itself when a young infant reaches for a dangling toy may later affect his ability to right himself, crawl, and walk.

Now let's think of the baby who reaches out for a dangling toy. An infant who is not developing in a typical manner might always reach for a toy or other object with his right hand, but seldom or never with his left hand. He might also turn his head in response to the sound of a rattling toy on his left side, but not in response to a toy on his right side.

As an infant gets older, these asymmetries may become more pronounced. For instance, when a child learns to right himself by turning from a back-lying position to a stomach-lying position, he may turn only to the left or only to the right. (See Chapter 5 to learn more about righting.) When a child starts to crawl, instead of moving his left and right leg in the same way, he may crawl with one leg while stepping with the other

Crossing the Midline

Throughout this chapter, we emphasize that an infant's symmetrical movement indicates that the two sides of his brain are developing equally well. Another means of detecting typical brain development is a child's ability to *cross the midline*—that is, his ability to extend each hand over the body's midline, which is an imaginary line that bisects the body into two equal halves.

At three to four months of age, a typical infant is able to bring his two hands together at the midline. A few months later, the infant will cross the midline, perhaps by using his right arm to reach for a toy on his left side. Crossing the midline is an important milestone in motor development because it signals that the left and right halves of the body are well integrated. Moreover, there is a clear indication that children who have problems crossing the midline experience developmental delays.

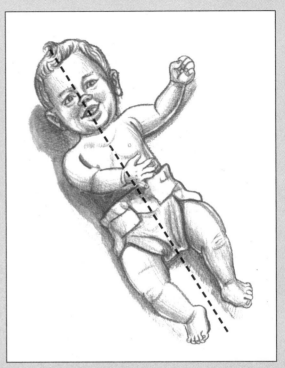

A Baby Crossing the Midline

leg. (To learn more about crawling, see Chapter 6.) As you would expect, his progression to walking can also be affected by this asymmetrical development.

Of course, only robots are completely symmetrical in structure and function. Everyone's movements are slightly asymmetrical at times. But asymmetries of position and motion should be brief. It is only when an asymmetry persists and hampers the baby's ability to appropriately perform certain tasks, from grasping objects to crawling and walking, that it becomes a cause for worry. A *persistent asymmetry*, which is a cause for concern, is very obvious, appears repeatedly, and lasts for at least a month. In some instances, persistent asymmetries last a lifetime.

WHAT YOU CAN DO

As discussed above, not all asymmetries signal a problem, but when they persist over a period of time, they are a cause for concern. Fortunately, it

The Moebius Mouth

Throughout this book, we explain how infant movement patterns can be used to detect the potential for autism or Asperger's syndrome far earlier in life than most experts believe possible. But in some children, a symptom called the *Moebius mouth* can serve as the very first signal that autism may develop.

Named after Paul Julius Moebius, the German neurologist who first clearly described this symptom in adults, Moebius mouth is one of a number of symptoms that together form the Moebius syndrome. The characteristic shape of a Moebius mouth involves a very flat lower lip and a tented, almost triangular upper lip. If you compare it with the mouth of a typically developing baby, you can see that the two are quite different. (See the figures below.)

Moebius mouth is associated with an abnormal function of cranial nerves VI and VII. The nerve impairment can cause lifetime facial paralysis, resulting not only in the characteristic mouth shape, but also in the inability to smile and, in some cases, the inability to blink or move the eyes from side to side. Because of the paralysis, which can exist to various degrees, it is sometimes difficult for an infant with Moe-

bius syndrome to close his mouth around the nipple when sucking. Some infants need to have their parents gently hold the lips around the nipple, and some have to use a special feeding device called a Haberman bottle.

Be aware that although Moebius mouth is sometimes linked to autism, not all children with Moebius have autism, and not all autistic people have the Moebius syndrome. Also be aware that although a Moebius mouth can sometimes be detected at birth, during the first few months of a child's life, it is sometimes difficult to distinguish this condition from a normal mouth. If it really is present, though, it will finally be apparent, and will persist throughout childhood and adulthood. The Moebius syndrome is a lifetime condition.

Do not be alarmed if your newborn seems to have a Moebius mouth. Only if the shape persists for at least a couple of months should you be concerned. Remember, too, that Moebius syndrome *alone* does not mean autism. But if this mouth shape is detected along with one or more of the problem motor behaviors described in this book, there is a strong likelihood that autism will eventually develop.

A Typical Infant Mouth

A Moebius Mouth With Tented Upper Lip

is easy to tell if your baby is exhibiting a persistent asymmetry. You can observe it in your own home without specialized equipment or professional advice. Just as important, you can take simple but important steps to encourage your infant's integration of the two halves of his body.

Observe and Keep Records

Good old observation is often overlooked these days. Now that we have gizmos and gadgets for just about everything, we are becoming increasingly dependent on machines for information about our bodies. While it's true that medical technology can be incredibly accurate, effective, and helpful, the best equipment in the world cannot replace your ability to watch your child and note what is happening.

Don't be upset if your child shows an asymmetrical movement for a brief period of time. Only if this asymmetry persists for at least a month should it be a cause for concern.

As you observe your baby, it is vital to keep a record of what you see. As already discussed, an asymmetry is considered persistent if it continues for at least a month, so you'll want to follow your child's behavior over time. Your records can be in the form of a written diary or journal (see the Observation Journal, which begins on page 131), or in the form of a photo/video diary. (Most of our research has been based on video diaries created when parents turned on a video camera and let it run for minutes at a time, recording their child's movements.) Try to update the journal as often as possible—at least once a week—so that you can track changes, and continue keeping the journal for several months, or even for the entire first year of your baby's life.

When observing your child, you are most likely to note any problems (or lack of them) if you focus on specific positions and movements. Some of the behaviors noted below have already been discussed in this chapter, while others have not yet been mentioned. All can provide valuable clues to your child's development.

- Compare the activity level of the left and right sides of your baby's body. Does it look like the limbs on one side of the body are more active than those on the other side? If so, is the same side (left or right) always the active one, or does this vary?

- Watch your baby's eyes. Does one eye tend to "get stuck" in the corner, close to your infant's nose? While this, by itself, is not a warning sign for autism, it may be significant if it appears in combination with other movement problems.

- If your child is old enough to choose the side on which he sleeps, note the side he selects. Is it always the same side? If so, is the side on which he sleeps also the one that is less active during his waking hours?

- At around three months of age, when your baby is lying on his back, does he bring his hands together? As explained in the inset on page 19, this indicates that the two sides of the body are becoming symmetrically integrated.

- At around seven months of age, does your baby ever cross one of his arms over his midline to the other side of his body? This is another important motor milestone. (See the inset on page 19.)

- If your baby is old enough to lift his head while lying on his stomach, observe how he accomplishes this. Does he lift his head while propping himself up with *both* forearms, or does he try to prop himself up with one arm only? If he tends to use only one arm, which arm does he use?

- If your baby is old enough to turn his head towards the sound of a rattling toy, note if he is as likely to turn his head toward a toy on his left as he is toward a toy on his right. If he turns his head toward one side only, in which direction does he turn?

- If your baby is old enough to reach for a toy, observe if he is as likely to reach for a toy with his right hand as he is with his left hand. If not, which arm does he tend to use?

- If your baby is old enough to right himself, note if he is able to turn in either direction. If not, in which direction does he turn?

- If your baby is old enough to crawl, watch to see if he uses both sides of his body equally. If not, which leg is doing the crawling, and which leg is either being dragged or "stepping" while the other one crawls?

- If your child has been walking for several weeks, is he able to coordinate the actions of his limbs and walk steadily without falling? When children start to walk, it can take them a few weeks to walk smoothly and steadily. If your child is still struggling after this time, note if he always falls to the same side, and how frequently he does so.

Clearly, the failure of a baby to, say, reach for a toy held to his left may indicate problems other than autism. The infant may be failing to see the object, or may be unable to reach with that arm. But if these behaviors exist—and especially if they repeatedly occur over a period of weeks—it is important to discover the root cause of the problem.

Encourage Symmetry

If through your observations you've noted that your child has one or more persistent asymmetries, be assured that there are many ways in which you can help stimulate his weaker side—the side that is less active. Here are some simple steps you can take:

- Stroke the palm of your baby's weak hand to elicit a grip. (See Figure 2.5.) Repeat this often during the day.

**Figure 2.5
Stimulating
Your Baby's Hand**

Stroke your baby's weaker hand to elicit a grip.

- Hold a toy—preferably one that makes a sound when moved—out to your baby so that he must extend one of his hands to grasp it. If you are trying to stimulate his right arm, stay on the right side of his body, but move the toy to different spots on the right side so that your baby is induced to move his arm in different directions. (See Figure 2.6.)

**Figure 2.6
Stimulating
Your Baby's Arm**

Hold a toy on your child's weaker side so he must extend his arm to grasp it.

- When your baby is seven to eight months old, use the same toy mentioned in the above exercise to induce your child to move his weaker arm over the midline of his body to the other side. (See Figure 2.7.)

**Figure 2.7
Stimulating Your Baby
to Cross the Midline**

Use a toy to encourage
your baby to cross
the midline.

- Use your hands to flex one of your baby's legs so that his knee is moved close to his stomach. (See Figure 2.8.) Then place one hand against the sole of his foot and let him exert force to push your hand away. Try this first with each limb separately, and then with both legs together.

**Figure 2.8
Strengthening
Your Baby's Legs**

Encourage your baby
to exert force against
your hand with his foot.

- Stimulate all of your baby's limbs—both his legs and his arms—by rubbing them gently with a cloth. (See Figure 2.9.) For maximum stimulation, alternate between rough and smooth cloth, and between warm and cool material. (To avoid frightening or hurting your baby, avoid using anything that's really hot or cold, or anything that's truly abrasive.)

**Figure 2.9
Stimulating
Your Baby's Limbs**

Gently rub a cloth on
your baby's limbs to
provide healthy stimulation.

- Move a toy or other object from side to side, up and down, and in a circle so that your baby can follow the object with his eyes. (See Figure 2.10.) Be sure to use the whole range of motion of both eyes.

**Figure 2.10
Stimulating
Your Baby's Eyes**

Move a toy or other
object from place to place
to exercise your baby's eyes.

- If you hold your baby when feeding him, alternate the arm with which you hold him. (See Figure 2.11.) This will stimulate both sides of his body.

**Figure 2.11
Alternate
Feeding Positions**

Encourage symmetric
development by
feeding your baby
on a different
side each time.

- When you place your baby in his crib, lay him on a different side each time. (See Figure 2.12.)

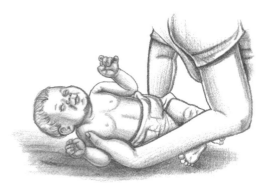

**Figure 2.12
Alternate
Sleeping Positions**

Stimulate both sides
of your baby's body by
laying him on a different
side each time.

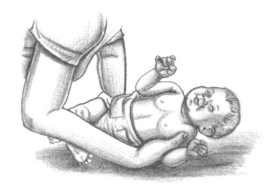

Seek Help

If you have observed persistent asymmetry in your infant, it's important to seek professional help—even if you are using the exercises just described to start dealing with his asymmetry. Begin by contacting your baby's pediatrician, who may be able to determine if your infant's problem is caused by neurological impairment or a physiological difficulty. Remember to bring the records of your observations so that you can give a complete account of your child's motor development. Detailed records can be very helpful to a concerned physician.

If your baby's doctor doesn't respond satisfactorily to your concerns, don't hesitate to seek a second opinion. Chapter 9 will help you locate a physician or therapist who can evaluate your infant's development and provide the assistance he needs.

You now know that typically, a child's motor skills develop symmetrically. When they do not, it signals a potential neurological disorder, and possibly, the beginning of autism. While this is likely to be frightening to the parent of a child whose behavior is asymmetric, the fact is that this behavior allows you to detect problems and seek treatment earlier than most experts believe possible.

But asymmetry isn't the only warning sign visible to the observant parent. The next chapter explores reflexes gone astray, another means of identifying the neurological damage that can signal autism.

CHAPTER 3

*R*eflexes

A newborn baby does not have the neurological maturity to react to the world with voluntary movements. She cannot sit up, crawl, or walk. Instead, she responds to the world with reflexes, which are behaviors that are programmed into her nervous system before she is born. As the baby grows and develops, some of these inborn reflexes fade, and some remain. At the same time, the growing infant acquires new reflexes as a function of neurological development.

A healthy infant's reflexes—the ones she has at birth and the new ones she develops over time—are fairly predictable, making them a valuable means of detecting possible neurological problems. This chapter first explains the importance of reflexes and examines various types of these involuntary responses. It then discusses reflex problems that may signal autism or Asperger's syndrome.

THE IMPORTANCE OF REFLEXES

In the womb, the baby is protected from the world she is about to enter. Once she is born and leaves the safety and comfort of the womb, she is immediately exposed to an unfamiliar world. In order to survive, she must breathe for herself, obtain nourishment from breast or bottle, and protect herself from strong stimuli, such as harsh light. Fortunately, she is equipped with an inborn set of responses that we call reflexes.

Reflexes are fixed movement patterns that occur automatically in response to specific stimuli. For instance, in response to a very bright light, an infant will close her eyes. In response to a painful stimulus, an infant will withdraw her arms or legs. The infant has no choice; she must respond this way. This means that the higher levels of the brain are not involved. Indeed, these early reflexes are located in the brain stem, which controls more primitive vital functions, such as breathing. (To learn more about the brain, see page 42 in Chapter 4.)

Every baby has the same reflexes. These movements are identical in their patterns and in the approximate time of their appearance. That is why they are useful for assessing a baby's development. If a reflex fails to appear at the right time or fails to disappear at the right time, this is a clear signal that the child's development has gone astray.

UNDERSTANDING REFLEXES

At birth, an infant has a repertoire of reflexes already programmed into her nervous system. Most of these reflexes disappear during baby's first year.

A reflex takes place in response to a stimulation of the *peripheral nerves*—the nerves that run to your spinal cord and brain stem from other parts of your body. Sensory receptors detect the stimulus, and sensory nerve fibers relay the information to the central nervous system—the spinal cord and brain. Different nerve fibers then conduct the command *away* from the central nervous system back to the peripheral nerves, resulting in a reflexive action. In other words, each reflex is a kind of "neural loop" that ensures a quick, automatic response to specific stimuli.

An example of a very simple reflex is the knee jerk, which just about everyone has experienced during a doctor's visit. To activate this reflex, a stimulus in the form of a tap is applied to the area just below the knee. The tap activates sensory receptors in the patella tendon, which sends an impulse to the spinal cord. Information is then relayed back to the leg, causing the lower leg to quickly "jerk" forward in a reflexive action. This reflex helps maintain a standing posture.

When a baby is born, she already has what are called *neonatal reflexes* or *primitive reflexes*—reflexes that developed during uterine life and are apparent at birth. Most of these reflexes, like the sucking reflex, disappear during the first year of life as they are inhibited by higher centers of the brain. Others, like the blink reflex, should remain throughout life. (See the inset on page 34 for a complete list of reflexes in the newborn.)

In some cases, reflexes work together to achieve a certain goal. These are referred to as *allied reflexes*. For instance, when touched on her cheek or the corner of her mouth, an infant exhibits the *rooting reflex* by turning her head toward the stimulus (the touch), opening her mouth, and searching for a nipple. Once the nipple is in her mouth, she exhibits the *sucking reflex* by sucking forcefully and swallowing. Together, these two allied reflexes allow the infant to obtain nourishment.

As a baby grows and has various experiences, she also acquires new reflexes, which are programmed into her nervous system as the result of a stimulus being repeated again and again. For example, after a baby has been fed with a bottle several times, the visual stimulus of seeing the bottle is enough to make her anticipate receiving the bottle again. In response to the stimulus, she reaches out, grasps the bottle, and opens her mouth. Because this response is not only learned but also combines several reflexes in response to a certain stimulus, we refer to it as a *learned allied reflex*.

One reflex, the *symmetric tonic neck reflex* (STNR), is not present when an infant is born, but appears slightly later in infancy, at about four to six months of age. This reflex is triggered by either extension (stretching) or flexion (bending) of the infant's head. When the infant's head is extended backwards, it results in straightening of the arms and bending of the legs. (See Figure 3.1A.) When the infant's head is bent forward, with the chin approaching the chest, it causes bending of the arms and straightening of the legs. (See Figure 3.1B.) Although this reflex is necessary to initially get an infant into the proper position for crawling, it typically disappears by the ninth month of life. (To learn more about the STNR and crawling, see page 60 in Chapter 6.)

**Figure 3.1
The Symmetric
Tonic Neck Reflex**

A. When a baby's head is extended backwards, the arms straighten and the legs bend.

B. When a baby's head is bent forward, the arms bend and the legs straighten.

**Figure 3.2
The Parachute Reflex**
When a typical
child falls, she extends
her arms forward.

Another reflex that is not present at birth but develops later in infancy is the *parachute reflex*. This reflex, which appears anywhere between six and nine months of age, causes a child to extend her arms forward when she feels she's falling, as if to break the fall. (See Figure 3.2.) If you hold a typical infant so that she's suspended in the air, and then lower her to make her feel as if she's falling, you will see her throw her arms out in a reflex movement that protects her chest and head from hitting the floor.

WHEN REFLEXES GO ASTRAY

You now know what a reflex is, and you know about the reflexes with which an infant is born, as well as some of the reflexes she normally acquires as she matures and develops. It's important to understand that infant reflexes have a preset schedule. Each one is supposed to appear at a certain time, with some appearing in the womb, some at birth, and some later. Once the baby gains more control of her movements, most of these reflexes are no longer needed and should disappear. When infant reflexes don't stick to their schedule—when they either don't appear when they should, or they don't disappear when they should—we say that they have gone astray. Reflexes are also said to go astray when they cannot be properly combined as allied reflexes to allow the baby to achieve a certain goal. Any of these problems can be reflected in abnormal movement patterns early in life, signaling neurological damage and the potential for autism or related disorders.

If reflexes fail to appear or disappear when they should, a baby may have trouble mastering a range of motor activities, from righting to walking.

One reflex gone astray was observed in an eight-month-old child who was later diagnosed with Asperger's syndrome. When trying to right herself—to turn from lying on her back to lying on her stomach, with her arms supporting her chest—this child began with her left arm outstretched and her head turned toward the outstretched arm. Typically, an infant turns in the direction to which her head is turned. But in this case, the child turned to the opposite side (the right) and used *bridge righting*— an atypical form of righting in which the child arches her back, thus making contact with the ground with only her heels and head. When the baby reached her final prone position, the left arm was still outstretched and therefore couldn't support her chest. We were puzzled by this baby's actions until we realized that her original posture was the asymmetric tonic neck reflex (ATNR) pattern. The child's retention of this reflex, which should have been inhibited months earlier, prevented her from properly righting herself. (See pages 52 to 54 for more about bridge righting.)

We also noted persistence of the asymmetric tonic neck reflex in an eleven-month-old child who was starting to stand and walk. This child, too, had her head turned toward her outstretched arm. As a result, the child overbalanced when walking, falling in the direction of the outstretched arm. (See Chapter 8 for more about walking.)

Another reflex gone astray was seen in infants who were learning to sit independently. Many of these children—all of whom were later diagnosed as autistic—were unable to maintain an upright position at an age when the typical child can remain seated while playing with toys. More important to this discussion is that when these children fell, they did not exhibit the parachute reflex by breaking their fall with their hands. Instead, such an infant would tumble onto her face, keeping her arms in a passive position alongside her body during the fall. (To learn more about sitting, see Chapter 7.)

The parachute reflex, which typically appears at eight or nine months of age, causes a baby to extend her arms forward when falling. A child who lacks this reflex will keep her arms in a passive position when tumbling forward.

Finally, we have found that some autistic-to-be children are unable to combine allied reflexes to achieve a specific goal. One example of failed allied reflexes was seen in a six-month-old child who was being bottle-fed. Instead of reaching out and grasping her bottle, as would a typical infant of that age, this infant sat with her arm resting passively on the chair. This behavior continued long after infancy. When the child was four years old, her hands would grope each other in front of her chest, failing to grasp the spoon. She did, however, open her mouth when the spoon was showed to her, indicating that the problem lay more in the coordination of the movements of her hands than in learning that the spoon meant food. The child turned out to have severe autism.

In the chapters that follow, you will return to some of the examples mentioned only briefly above, and will learn more about righting, sitting,

Reflexes in the Newborn

As explained on page 29, infants are born with certain reflexes already programmed into their nervous system. These *neonatal, primitive,* or *infant reflexes* are part of a normal newborn evaluation, as they show that the baby's neurological system is developing normally. It is important to recognize that it is not always easy to demonstrate these reflexes and that not all babies show them all of the time, so you may not be able to trigger every single reflex in your child. Moreover, it is not safe for a nonprofessional to trigger certain reflexes, as this can harm the baby if done incorrectly. A trained professional, however, can safely elicit the following responses in a typically developing newborn.

Asymmetric Tonic Neck Reflex (ATNR). Sometimes called the *fencer response,* this reflex is activated when a baby's head is turned to one side while she is lying on her back. As the head is turned, the arm and leg on that same side extend or straighten, while the opposite limbs bend in a pose that has been compared to that of a fencer. Note that a typical child shows the ATNR whether his head is turned to the right or to the left. No preference is exhibited for one direction over the other. This reflex is usually inhibited by four to six months of age. (See figure below.)

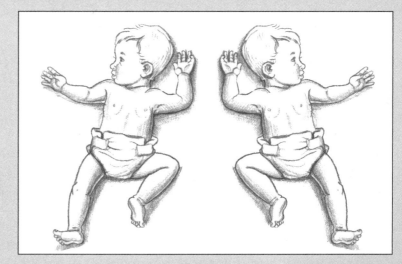

**Asymmetric Tonic
Neck Reflex (ATNR)**

Babinski Reflex. This response is triggered when a finger or other object strokes the sole of the baby's foot upward from the heel, across the ball of the foot. In response, the infant hyperextends her toes, fanning them out. This reflex usually fades between the sixth and ninth months. (See figure below.)

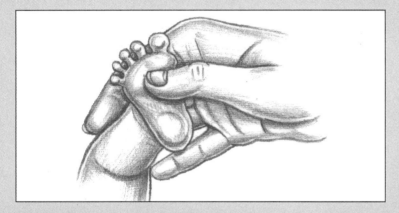

Babinski Reflex

Blink Reflex. This response occurs when a bright light is shone directly into a baby's eyes. The infant closes her eyes, showing a reflex that should persist throughout her life.

Galant Reflex. The Galant reflex is activated when a baby is placed on her stomach or lightly supported under her abdomen, and then gently stroked to one side of the spinal column, from her neck to her lower back. In response, the back curves sideways, away from the stimulus. This reflex disappears between the first and sixth months. (See figure below.)

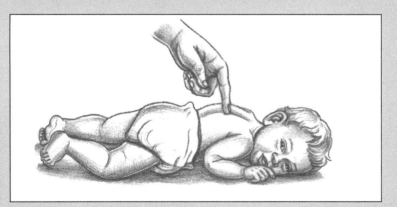

Galant Reflex

Grasping Reflex. This response, also known as the *palmar reflex,* is triggered when a finger or other object is placed in a baby's open palm. In response to the touch, the baby grasps or grips the object, gripping even more strongly if the object is pulled away. This reflex usually disappears when the baby is about six months of age. (See figure below.)

Grasping Reflex

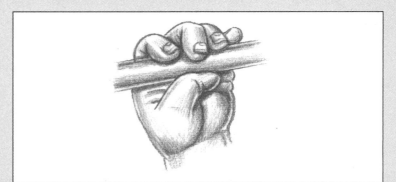

Moro Reflex. Also called the *startle reflex,* the Moro reflex is triggered when a baby is startled by a loud noise or when her head falls backward or quickly changes position. In these potentially threatening situations, the reflex causes the baby to first symmetrically spread her arms and legs out wide and extend her neck, and then pull her arms back across her body in a clasping motion. The Moro reflex usually fades between the third and sixth months. (See figure below.)

Moro Reflex

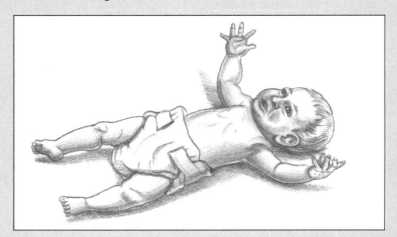

Stepping Reflex. This reflex can be triggered by holding the baby under her arms, with her head supported, and allowing her feet to touch a flat surface. Her response is to move her feet as if to walk. The stepping reflex usually disappears when the infant is two to four months of age. (See figure on right.)

Stepping Reflex

Sucking Reflex. The sucking reflex is triggered when a finger or nipple is placed in a newborn's mouth. In response, the baby sucks forcefully and rhythmically on the finger or nipple, swallowing in coordination with her sucking. Like the rooting reflex, this response disappears somewhere between the third and fourth months of life. (See figure on right.)

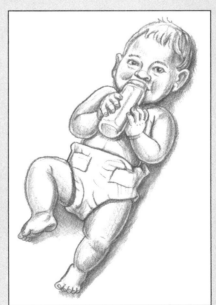

Sucking Reflex

Rooting Reflex. This response is stimulated when a finger touches an infant's cheek or the corner of her mouth. The baby then turns her head toward the stimulus, opening her mouth and searching (rooting) for the stimulus. The rooting reflex, which facilitates the nursing process, is usually inhibited by the third or fourth month. (See figure below.)

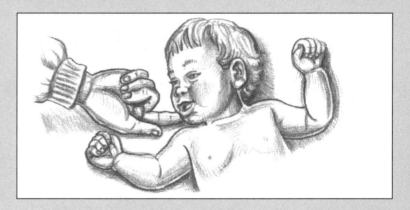

Rooting Reflex

crawling, and walking. The important point to keep in mind is that the skills which a baby learns in the first year of life are inextricably tied to infant reflexes. When these reflexes go astray, the baby cannot develop in a typical manner.

WHAT YOU CAN DO

As discussed earlier in this chapter, during a child's first year of life, her reflexes should appear—and in most cases fade—according to a fairly predictable time table. If they fail to appear when they should, if they persist instead of disappearing as they should, or if other reflex-related problems occur, there is cause for concern.

Observe and Keep Records

Good old observation is often overlooked these days. While it's true that medical technology can be incredibly accurate, effective, and helpful, the best equipment in the world cannot replace your ability to watch your child and note what is happening.

As you observe your baby, it is vital to keep a record of what you see. Your records can be in the form of a written diary or journal (see the

Observation Journal on page 131), or in the form of a photo/video diary. (Most of our research has been based on video diaries.) Try to update the journal at least once a week so that you can track changes, and continue keeping the journal for several months, or even for the entire first year of your baby's life. Especially watch for instances of reflexes gone astray, as described on pages 32 through 33. Keep in mind that typical reflexes, such as the Babinski response, are often difficult to "catch." Once the stimulus occurs, its effect is usually momentary. But when a reflex goes astray and results in a problem such as atypical righting, the behavior is often easy to observe and note as long as you know what you're looking for.

If you suspect that your child's reflexes have gone astray, be sure to contact a professional for an accurate evaluation. Do not try to elicit the reflexes yourself, as in some cases, this may cause the baby harm.

Seek Help

If you feel that your child's motor skills may signal reflex-related problems, it's important to seek professional help, as only a professional can

---

Understanding Reflexes of Approach and Avoidance

If you have spent time with older children who have autism, you may be familiar with the avoidance behavior they often show in social situations. In videotapes, we have seen an autistic child avoid looking at an adult who walked toward her, and stick her fingers in her ears so that she wouldn't hear what the adult was saying. Similarly, when approached on the playground, one child covered her eyes to cut off visual contact with the schoolmate who was walking towards her.

When a person reflexively responds to a stimulus by avoiding it, we refer to the response as a *reflex of avoidance*. When an individual reflexively responds to a stimulus by approaching or accepting it, we call it a *reflex of approach*. The above examples, of course, involve children's interactions with other people—a type of behavior that does not begin until the child is two or three years old. But if older autistic chil-

dren show such a great imbalance in these social reflexes, isn't it possible that infants might show an imbalance of motor reflexes?

Many infant reflexes can easily be categorized as reflexes of approach or avoidance. For instance, the grasping reflex, which causes the child to grip an object that's placed in her palm, is a reflex of approach because it increases the child's contact with that object. On the other hand, the blinking reflex, which causes the child to close her eyes in response to a bright light, is a reflex of avoidance. As of yet, no one has tested potentially autistic infants to determine if their reflexes of avoidance are dominant over those of approach. But based on our observations, we believe that further study will show an observable imbalance of reflexes in these infants, and that this imbalance may prove to be an important factor in identifying and understanding autism.

accurately evaluate a baby's reflexes. A good first contact is your baby's pediatrician, who may be able to determine if your child's struggle is being caused by a physical problem or is a possible sign of neurological impairment. Remember to bring the records of your observations so that you can give a complete account of your child's development. Detailed records can be very helpful to a concerned physician.

If your baby's doctor doesn't respond satisfactorily to your concerns, don't hesitate to seek a second opinion. A developmental behavioral pediatrician, who is trained in the assessment and treatment of children with developmental delays and disabilities, might be better equipped to evaluate your child's motor development. (See Chapter 9 for other ideas.)

You now know that typically, a newborn's reflexes appear and fade in a predictable manner. When they do not, it signals a potential neurological disorder, and possibly, the beginning of autism. But reflexes gone astray aren't the only warning signs visible to the observant parent. The next chapter explores the Ladder of Motor Development, another means of identifying the neurological impairment that can signal autism.

CHAPTER 4

*T*he Ladder of Motor Development

The central task of a baby's first year of life is to achieve *motor independence*—the ability to walk around without help from others. By the end of the first year, or soon afterwards, the typical baby has pretty much reached this goal. He can walk on his own and he has control over the rest of his limbs, so that he is free to act and to move around.

An infant's progression from relative helplessness to motor independence can be seen as a transition from being completely horizontal (lying down) to being completely vertical (standing and walking). Each step along the way—each new capability that is acquired, allowing greater freedom of movement—is called a *motor development stage*. Like rungs of a ladder, every stage builds on the stage below it, and leads to another stage above it. That is why we call this transition process the *Ladder of Motor Development*.

As you know, this process doesn't happen overnight. There are many skills that a baby needs to acquire before he masters walking, and the skills are developed one at a time, with each one more complex than the one before. As a baby learns to use his body, he tries many different movements, and the path is very much one of trial and error. But the order of the stages remains fixed.

Every baby on the face of the Earth, regardless of race, gender, or background, climbs the Ladder of Motor Development. In most cases, even the autistic child climbs this ladder and reaches motor independence. But in the case of a child with autism, the process itself generally does not conform to that of the nonautistic child. That's what makes the Ladder of Motor Development so useful to the parent who's trying to determine if his child is at risk for autism. Only after you understand normal infant motor development can you identify abnormal development.

This chapter first briefly examines how the brain's development facilitates the Ladder of Motor Development. It then examines the ladder itself, explaining how infants generally move toward motor independence during the first year of life.

NEUROLOGICAL DEVELOPMENT

When an infant is born, his brain is composed of over 100 billion nerve cells, or *neurons,* which are connected through electrochemical structures called *synapses.* It is the neurons that carry messages from the body's sense receptors (the eyes, ears, nose, etc.) to the central nervous system (the spinal cord and brain). Many of the connecting synapses are generated after birth as a result of environmental stimulation. As new synapses form, they organize the brain, enabling its various portions to develop sequentially—from the brain stem upwards—until the brain is mature. (See the inset below to learn more about the anatomy of the brain.) Throughout life, the nervous system maintains its ability to modify its synaptic connections, but this is done with greatest ease during the earliest period of development, when the brain is most "plastic."

The Structure of the Brain

The brain is the control center of the *central nervous system,* which also includes the spinal cord. In the text above, you learned that different centers of the infant's brain develop at different times, until the brain is completely mature. To better appreciate the importance of this process, it's helpful to have some knowledge of the major segments of the brain and their various functions.

The three main components of the brain—the cerebrum, the cerebellum, and the brain stem—each perform specific tasks.

The *cerebrum* is the largest and most developmentally advanced part of the human brain. It is divided into two relatively symmetrical halves called *hemispheres.* In general, the right hemisphere controls the left side of the body, and the left hemisphere controls the right side of the body.

Each hemisphere of the brain is divided into four lobes—the frontal lobe, parietal lobe, occipital lobe, and temporal lobe. The *frontal lobe* is involved in reasoning, planning, organizing, and problem solving. It also plays a part in controlling emotional responses, expressive language, word association, and motor activity, as well as in inhibiting impulsive and reflexive actions. The *parietal lobe* is involved in visual attention, touch perception, the manipulation of objects, goal-directed voluntary motion, and the integration of senses necessary for understanding concepts. The *occipital lobe* processes visual information, and helps in the visual recognition of shapes and colors. Finally, the *temporal lobe* is responsible for processing auditory information—information that is heard. It is also involved in vision, in sorting new information, and in forming new memories.

The *cerebellum* plays an important role in the integration of sensory perception and movement. In essence, it uses constant feedback from the senses to fine-tune motor activity.

The *brain stem* is the lowest extension of the brain. It forms a bridge between the cerebrum

As an infant develops and interacts with his environment, three important systems of feedback develop as well, making it possible for him to learn new motor skills. Each of these feedback mechanisms helps the brain integrate and interpret sensory stimulation.

The *tactile system,* which involves the nerves under the skin, provides the brain with information about light touch, pressure, temperature, and pain. In its most basic form, this system enables a sense of contact with the ground.

The *proprioceptive system* consists of nerves that monitor internal changes in the body brought about by movement and muscular activity. Proprioceptors found in muscles and tendons convey information that is used to coordinate motor activity.

The *vestibular system* involves structures in the inner ear that detect movement and changes in the position of the head. As the body moves,

and the spinal cord, and permits messages to pass to and from the cerebellum. The brain stem is also responsible for those involuntary neurological functions necessary for survival—breathing, digestion, heart rate, and blood pressure.

Even this simplified overview of the major sections of the brain shows the complexity of this organ. It also gives clues as to how damage to specific portions of the brain can result in atypical behavior. For instance, damage to the frontal lobes—the lobes that inhibit reflexive action—can cause the rooting and sucking reflexes to be triggered in an adult simply by touching the person's face near the mouth.

The Human Brain

The human brain has three major sections—the cerebrum, cerebellum, and brain stem. Each cerebral hemisphere is, in turn, composed of four lobes.

Parietal Lobe

Frontal Lobe

Cerebrum

Temporal Lobe

Brain Stem

Occipital Lobe

Cerebellum

Because the frontal lobes are also is involved in motor activity, damage can affect the individual's motor function, as well, with impairment of the right lobe affecting the left side of the body, and impairment of the left lobe affecting the body's right side.

All of the components of the brain must mature and work together in order for an infant to develop not just motor skills, but also many other skills—language, reasoning, etc.—necessary for independence. When some of these components fail to mature as they should, the result can be the motor and behavioral problems often associated with autism.

this system allows it to maintain balance, position, and vertical orientation in space. (See page 70 to learn more about the vestibular system.)

It is important to understand that brain development moves from the simple to the complex, so that as the nervous system matures, higher centers of the brain are recruited. The brain centers that control the sensory-motor aspects of development are recruited first. Later, the centers of the brain responsible for language and learning are activated. The last regions of the brain to be developed are those that regulate emotion and those involved in abstract thought. Because each new stage is built upon the previous one, a disorganized motor system may hamper the development of higher-level learning.

CLIMBING THE LADDER OF MOTOR DEVELOPMENT

During the first year of life, infant reflexes fade as the infant masters righting, crawling, sitting, walking, and other motor skills.

As you learned in Chapter 3, at birth, before a baby has acquired motor skills, he responds to stimuli with *reflexes*—responses that are programmed into his nervous system before he is born, and over which he has no control. These programmed behaviors, such as the sucking reflex, enable the baby to survive until he is able to move voluntarily, at which point, the reflexes are inhibited by the frontal lobe. (See Chapter 3 to learn more about reflexes.)

For most infants, the physical milestones that mark the first year of motor development are fairly predictable. The remainder of this chapter provides an overview of these milestones.

In the first few days after he is born, the baby, when not held, lies with his whole body in contact with the ground. In this position, his ability to move is extremely limited. When he is lying on his back, though, he has greater freedom to move his arms and legs than he does when lying on his stomach.

In just four to six short weeks, when lying on his stomach, the baby makes his initial attempts to raise his head from the surface. (See Figure 4.1.) At first, he raises his head an inch or so. This work is done mostly by the

**Figure 4.1
The Infant Raises His
Head From the Floor**

Four to six weeks
after birth, an infant
begins to raise his
head off the floor.

extensor muscles of the neck and the upper back. Thus begins the process of "peeling" the body away from its binding connection with the ground.

Over the next week or two, the infant's head steadily inches upward and becomes the first body segment to assume a vertical position. (See Figure 4.2.). Then his arms and hands start to participate as well, bearing some of the weight of the chest, which by now is also partly released from contact with the surface. Somewhere between eight and twelve weeks of age,

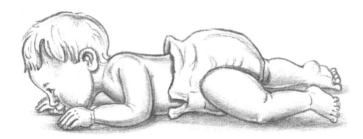

Figure 4.2
The Infant's Head
Inches Higher

Eventually, an infant's head becomes the first body part to assume a vertical position.

the baby, when lying on his stomach, achieves his first degree of freedom of movement. With his raised head supported by his chest and arms, the baby is able to look around and explore his environment. (See Figure 4.3.) From this point on, the baby moves through successive milestones, each of which incorporates his previous skills and adds new components to them.

Figure 4.3
The Infant Begins
to Look Around

As his head moves higher and becomes better supported by chest and arms, an infant begins to look around.

At about four months of age, the baby begins *righting*—rolling from his back to his stomach. A short time after the baby reaches this milestone, he raises himself up on all fours in preparation for crawling, and pretty soon, he takes his first crawling "steps." At this stage, the arms and thighs are essentially vertical (see Figure 4.4); the head position is voluntarily controlled by the baby; and the torso, although still horizontal, is released from its restrictive contact with the ground.

Figure 4.4 Crawling
Between six and ten months of age, an infant raises himself up on all fours and begins to crawl.

About six months after birth, the baby learns to sit independently. This can be viewed as the halfway point both chronologically and in a positional sense, because although the upper body is upright, the legs are still horizontal. (See Figure 4.5.) For the first time, the baby's arms are freed from the task of bearing the weight of his body. This allows the infant to manipulate objects within a wider range, coordinating the movements of his eyes, head, and hands. Numerous books and papers have been written on this unique feature of ours—the freedom of our upper limbs to manipulate our environment.

Figure 4.5 Sitting
At about six months of age, a baby learns to sit up without outside support.

Figure 4.6 Standing

At eight to ten months of age, an infant stands for the first time—usually supporting himself with furniture until he gains confidence and balance.

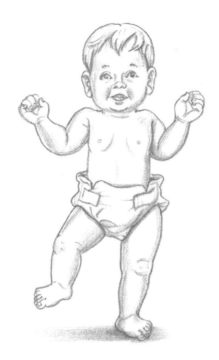

Figure 4.7 Walking

Between eleven and thirteen months of age, the typical infant takes his first steps.

In the next two stages, the baby completes the process of assuming a vertical position. At eight to ten months of age, a baby normally pulls himself up to a standing position for a brief period of time. Usually, he first supports himself using furniture or other surrounding objects for a period of several seconds to a few minutes (see Figure 4.6), and then sinks (or falls) back to the floor. Once he gains confidence, he stands on his own.

The final rung of the ladder of motor development is walking independently. (See Figure 4.7.) All of the assimilated skills are interwoven into this final skill, which the typical baby begins mastering somewhere between eleven and thirteen months of age.

As mentioned earlier, the process of gaining motor independence moves from the simple to the complex. In the early stages of development, when the baby is stationary, his motor behavior is relatively simple and his vocabulary of movements is limited. As the baby's motor behavior matures, each new stage—each new rung on the Ladder of Motor Development—is built upon the previous one through the addition of a new

As a baby moves up the Ladder of Motor Development, each new skill builds on previous skills until he reaches the ladder's zenith by learning to walk independently.

Understanding the Difference Between Gross and Fine Motor Skills

A motor skill is an action that involves movement of the body's muscles. These skills are generally divided into two groups. *Gross motor skills* involve the larger movements of the arms, legs, and feet, or the entire body. Sitting, crawling, standing, walking, and running all involve gross motor skills. *Fine motor skills* are small actions, usually performed by the thumb and a finger or fingers in coordination with the eyes. Activities that use fine motor skills include drawing, writing, lacing a shoe, and buttoning a shirt.

While some autistic children have excellent fine motor skills, others show delays in developing these skills, and become agitated when instructed to write, lace a pair of shoes, or perform other detail-oriented tasks. But this book focuses on gross motor activity—sitting, crawling, walking, etc. Why? It is through the development of these large-scale coordinated activities—some of which are performed long before a child acquires any fine motor abilities—that children can show the earliest signs of potential neurological problems. In other words, gross motor skills appear to be the key to detecting autism in the earliest possible stage of a child's life.

component. We cannot overemphasize the fact that it's vital for *every* baby to reach *every* rung on the ladder. If he skips one, it's not like skipping a grade. Rather, it may signal a problem in his overall development, and should be promptly addressed.

During the first year of life, the typically developing baby climbs the Ladder of Motor Development, moving from neurological immaturity and relative physical helplessness to a point where he can sit up, stand, and eventually walk on his own. Throughout the year, as he reaches each new rung on the ladder, the baby builds on skills he's already developed to further enhance his freedom of movement.

Each of the next four chapters in this book provides a detailed description of one motor stage and its characteristics. Most important, it compares that stage as experienced by typically developing babies with the same stage experienced by babies who were later diagnosed with autism or Asperger's syndrome. This will not only give you a new window on the process of motor development, but will also provide a simple means of determining if your baby is developing in a healthy way, or if he may need help in climbing the Ladder of Motor Development.

CHAPTER 5

*R*ighting

In the previous chapter, you learned that in the first year of life, a child achieves motor independence by climbing the Ladder of Motor Development. She may begin as a relatively helpless being, able to respond to the world only through reflexive actions. But by the end of the year, she should be able to sit at will; to crawl; and, give or take a few weeks, to start taking her first independent steps.

The gateway to motor independence is the process of *righting*. As first described in Chapter 4, this action involves the baby turning independently from lying on her back to lying on her stomach. Without this skill, a baby is unable to assume the necessary prone position for more advanced activities such as crawling, sitting independently, standing, and walking. Just as important, we have found that infants who are unable to perform righting properly—or at all—often have neurological problems that might later be diagnosed as autism or Asperger's syndrome.

This chapter begins by discussing the importance of righting, and examines how righting is performed by a typically developing baby. It then describes righting difficulties that may signal more serious problems. Finally, it guides you in helping your child reach this rung on the Ladder of Motor Development.

THE IMPORTANCE OF RIGHTING

A baby's first means of locomotion is crawling. In order to crawl, she must first achieve a prone position. In other words, she must learn to turn onto her stomach.

It's vital to be aware that a baby's first attempts to release herself from the floor usually occur at four to six weeks of age—some time before she begins the righting process. At this early stage, when the baby is lying on her stomach, she will try to raise her head from the floor. At first, the arms and chest are not recruited, making the process hard work. Often after a few attempts, the baby gives up and returns her head to the floor, sometimes crying in frustration. Nevertheless, she continues to work at it, and through this process, she strengthens her neck and upper chest muscles.

At eight to twelve weeks of age, the typically developing baby can support her chest with her arms, which are pointed forward like the paws of an animal. By now, her head is fully vertical. And because most of her sense organs—her eyes, nose, ears, and mouth—are located in her head,

---

Figure 5.1
Early Typical Righting

The typical infant masters an early form of righting at around four months of age. At this stage, righting starts with a turning of the head followed by a corkscrew rotation that begins with the legs.

A. Typical righting starts with a tilting and rotation of the baby's head.

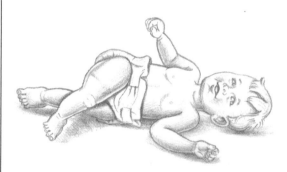

B. Corkscrew rotation begins as one leg crosses the body.

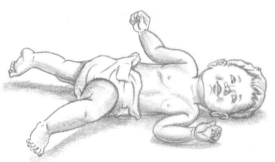

C. Corkscrew rotation moves from bottom to top as the pelvis rotates in the direction of the head.

D. As the turn progresses, baby's knee touches the floor.

E. When the turn is complete, the baby is in a supported position, ready to crawl.

she has a new freedom to look around and a dramatically enhanced ability to understand and respond to her environment. It is from this position that the baby will start to crawl, and it is to this position that the infant must arrive at the end of the righting process.

UNDERSTANDING THE NORMAL RIGHTING PROCESS

The beginnings of righting can be seen as early as four months of age. When the baby is lying on her back, typical righting starts with a tilting of the head backwards, accompanied by a rotation of the head to one side. (See Figure 5.1A.) The baby then brings the opposite leg across her body, following the direction of the head. (See Figure 5.1B.) This starts a corkscrew motion, which next causes the pelvis to rotate in the direction of the head. (See Figures 5.1C and D.) The corkscrew motion continues all the way up the body until the baby is lying on her stomach, with her head

A. As always, typical righting starts with a tilting and rotation of the baby's head.

Figure 5.2
Mature Typical Righting

Like early righting, mature righting begins with a turning of the baby's head. In this case, though, rotation of the baby's body begins at the shoulders and moves downwards, towards the child's legs. The final position leaves the baby balanced and ready to crawl.

B. In mature righting, the segment-by-segment rotation of the body starts with the shoulders and moves down the infant's body.

C. When the turn is complete, the baby is ready to crawl.

upright and her chest supported by her arms. In this final position, the leg that initiated the turn is flexed and in position to accept the baby's weight as she starts to crawl. (See Figure 5.1E.)

As a baby develops, she uses a more mature form of righting. The new form also begins with a backwards tilting and sideways rotation of the head, followed by a segment-by-segment rotation. This time, though, the rotation starts in the shoulders, rather than the legs, and works its way down the infant's body. (See Figures 5.2 A, B, and C.) As long as there is a corkscrew rotation present along with the other components—the head movement and the final position—the righting is that of a typically developing baby.

In most cases, when placed on her back, a ten-month-old baby will instantaneously right herself to a prone position. All of the movements she uses to get from one position to another, though, may not be apparent to the casual onlooker, because by that age, the movements will have been integrated to form a smooth, continuous pattern.

To sum it up, righting is made up of three basic components. The first component is the movement of the infant's head backward and toward the side to which she will turn. The second is the segmental corkscrew rotation of the body. Last, there is the final position: The baby lies on her stomach with her chest supported by her arms, head vertical, and one leg flexed, ready to crawl.

> Typical righting places a baby on her stomach, with her head upright and her chest supported by her arms. In this balanced position, she is ready to master her first means of locomotion—crawling.

PROBLEM RIGHTING

You now know how a typically developing baby rights herself so that she can assume a prone position at will. But our research has shown that not all babies acquire typical righting skills. Babies who fail to execute righting properly miss at least one of the three basic components just described, and often miss more than one. When trying to turn from back to stomach, many of these babies get stuck lying on their side. Sometimes the turn cannot be completed at all, and a caregiver must gently help the baby to turn over onto her stomach. Even when the baby is able to complete the turn on her own, she accomplishes it in a drastically different manner from that of the typical baby.

We first observed a form of problem righting that we refer to as *bridge righting* in an eight-month-old infant. If you look at Figure 5.3A, you will see an infant who is about to turn over to her right side. First, she is lying on her back with her head turned to the left, *away* from the direction in which she is about to turn. Notice that her left arm is extended. Instead of using her leg to create a corkscrew rotation, she arches her stomach upward, supporting herself on the heels of her feet and head and creating a "bridge." (See Figure 5.3B.) The extended arm becomes the lever that

> Although bridge righting gets a baby from her back to her stomach, it leaves her in an unsupported position, unable to crawl.

Figure 5.3 Bridge Righting

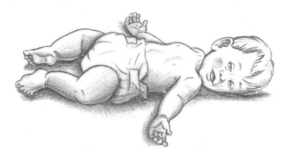

A. Bridge righting begins with baby's head turned away from the direction in which she is about to turn, and eyes fixated on her extended arm.

B. Instead of using a corkscrew type of rotation, the infant forms a "bridge" by arching her stomach upwards.

C. Using her arm as a lever, the baby begins her turn.

D. When the turn is complete, the baby is in an unsupported position, unable to crawl.

allows the body to turn over, as one unit, to the right—once again, *away* from the direction in which her head was originally facing. (See Figure 5.3C.) Thus, as the arm traces out its path, the head rotates along with it, as if the two were a single connected unit. Once the baby is on her stomach, the arm is still extended out to the side, rather than supporting the chest as it does in the usual final position of righting. (See Figure 5.3D.)

As you can see, bridge righting is drastically different from either of the typical methods of righting discussed earlier. Instead of positioning the baby so that she is balanced on all four limbs and ready to crawl, this process leaves the baby's chest on the floor, without support. Because this hampers the normal transition to crawling, it is disruptive to the Ladder of Motor Development, which builds each skill upon previously developed skills.

In a typically developing baby, the ATNR will appear sometimes on the left side, and sometimes on the right side. If a baby exhibits the ATNR on one side only, she has a form of persistent asymmetry. (See Chapter 2 for more information.)

One possible explanation for bridge righting is that the baby's efforts to right herself are being hampered by a partially *uninhibited reflex*—a reflex that did not disappear completely when it should have. In this case, the reflex in question is the asymmetric tonic neck reflex (ATNR), first mentioned in Chapter 3. This reflex is present at birth, but normally is inhibited (disappears completely) between four and six months of age. The ATNR is activated when a baby's head is turned to one side while she is lying on her back. As the head is turned, the arm and leg on the same side extend or straighten, while the opposite arm is raised alongside the back of the head in a pose that has been compared to that of a fencer who is about to lunge forward. (See Figure 5.4.) The head, the eyes, and the extended hand seem to be linked together, with the eyes focused on the hand. You've probably seen your baby lying in this distinctive posture in her crib. The extended arm and the fixation of the eyes, the trademarks of this reflex, are clearly visible in bridge righting, indicating that the ATNR is still affecting the baby's behavior to some degree. The extended arm prevents the infant from rotating in the direction in which the head is facing, and the baby compensates by employing the bridge position and rotating toward the other side instead. When she reaches her final position, the arm remains extended and therefore can't support the baby's chest as it does at the end of typical righting.

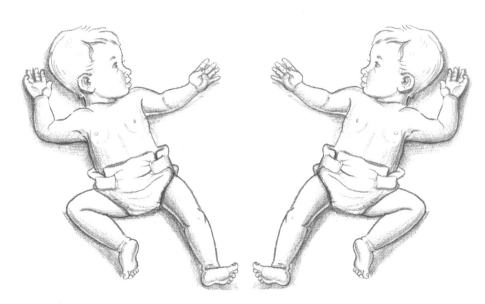

**Figure 5.4
The Asymmetric
Tonic Neck Reflex**

Activated when a baby's head is turned in either direction when lying on her back, this reflex has also been called the fencer response.

A number of autistic-to-be infants show a different but equally problematic pattern of righting, which we refer to as *U-righting.* In this pattern, the infant begins by pulling her thighs toward her tummy. Because her bent legs create an unstable position, she falls onto her side, where she becomes stuck. Her head doesn't lead the righting process, but remains in line with her body. In an effort to finish the turn, the baby raises both ends of her body—her legs and her head—creating a U-shape while still lying on her side. If you look at Figure 5.5A, you'll see that the baby's weight is now supported by a very small area located in the middle of her side. Because this area is so small, the infant falls onto her stomach, completing the turn. (See Figures 5.5B and C.) Like bridge righting, U-righting is lacking in corkscrew rotation, and fails to leave the baby in a balanced, supported position, ready for crawling.

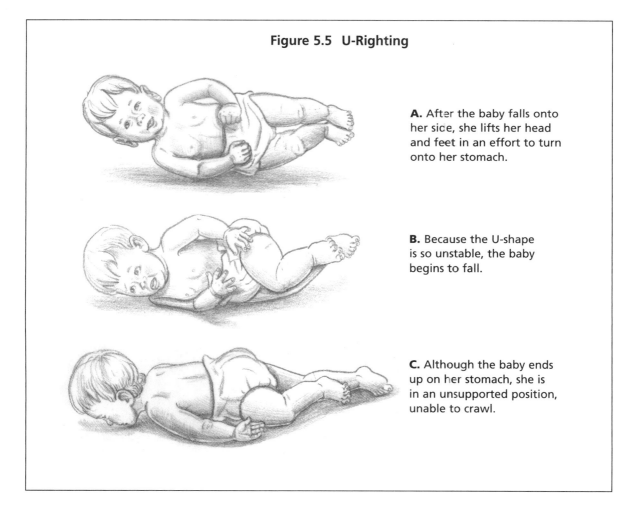

Figure 5.5 U-Righting

A. After the baby falls onto her side, she lifts her head and feet in an effort to turn onto her stomach.

B. Because the U-shape is so unstable, the baby begins to fall.

C. Although the baby ends up on her stomach, she is in an unsupported position, unable to crawl.

It's important to note that in the case of both bridge righting and U-righting, physicians often overlook movement patterns that can be warning signs of abnormal development. More often than not, since the infant is able to complete the turn, she is seen as "getting the job done," in the parlance of the physician. While this may be true, attention must also be paid to *how* she gets the job done. Since righting is a coordinated pattern in which reflexes and senses are integrated in a specific way, and not a random success after long hours of trying, there is a correct way for it to occur. Once parents and pediatricians are aware of this, they can begin to look for deviations from the correct method. It is our belief that such a deviation signals, at the very least, a disorganization in the reflexes of the infant.

A typical baby is able to right herself both towards the left and towards the right. The baby who rights herself to one side only may have a neurological problem.

Some children are able to right themselves to one side only—just to the right, for instance. While this may seem unimportant, a typical baby is able to right herself both towards the left and towards the right. When a child rights in one direction only, it is a sign of persistent asymmetry, and therefore a cause for concern.

The final variation in righting is its absence altogether. In other words, according to reports from a number of parents, some babies do not manage to right themselves at all. We have already pointed out that the motor development of your baby in the first year of her life can be compared to a ladder, the rungs of which the baby ascends as she grows. The absence of one of these stages is, therefore, an important fact to note.

WHAT YOU CAN DO

As you've learned, as early as four months of age, the typical baby starts the process of righting. But this does not occur with all children. If your child persists in having trouble righting herself, or does not try to right herself at all, it could be a cause for concern. For this reason, it is important to be aware of her progress.

Observe and Keep Records

You are in a unique position to see your baby move and change every day. You will know when she makes her first attempts to right herself, and if and when she masters the process of turning from her back to her stomach.

As you observe your infant, keep a record of what you see, as explained on page 21. Your records can be in the form of a written diary or journal (see the Observation Journal on page 131), or in the form of a photo/video diary. These records will give you an accurate picture of what is happening with your child, and will also enable you to provide helpful information to your child's doctor and other professionals.

When observing your infant's efforts to right herself, you are most likely to understand her progress if you look for the following typical positions and movements, and note if your child's movements differ from them.

- Look for the movements that herald the beginning of the righting process. Watch for the start of backwards head tilting and turning, and rocking from a back-lying position to a side-lying position. These movements may be brief and seemingly uncoordinated, but eventually, the typical baby starts stringing the separate components together.

- When your baby starts righting herself, note whether she is turning in the direction to which her head is facing (which is correct), or in the other direction (which is problematic).

- Try to distinguish the corkscrew rotation present in typical righting. The back of the head should remain in contact with the ground throughout the rotation. Moreover, an imaginary diagonal line should connect the hip joint and shoulder joint on the same side of the body as the baby is about to complete the turn. (See Figure 5.6.)

Figure 5.6
Noting the Baby's Corkscrew Rotation

In typical righting, when the baby is about to complete a turn to her left, an imaginary diagonal line connects the right shoulder and right hip joint.

- Note whether your baby rights herself to one side only, or if she is able to turn in both directions. During the first year of life, a baby should show little or no preference for one side over the other.

- Note if the final position of the turn involves the following components: erect head, chest supported by both arms, and leg that initiated turn in flexed position, ready to assume the body's weight.

Encourage Righting

If through your observations you've noted that your child is not righting in the typical manner—or is not righting at all—be assured that there are many ways in which you can help your baby master this motor milestone. Here are some simple steps you can take:

- Allow your baby to spend time on the floor each day, sometimes placing her on her tummy, and sometimes, on her back. Before starting this "exercise," make sure that your child is comfortable—not hungry, not wet, and not tired.

- Never physically push your child over to encourage her to right herself. Let her put the components of the righting process together on her own.

- When your baby is lying on her back, dangle a rattle or jingly toy to her right or left so that she has to reach to the side to get it. This may motivate her to turn towards the toy.

- Don't be alarmed if your baby doesn't right herself according to a precise schedule. The timetable for each child is different. But if your infant has not started the righting process by eight months of age, you should consult with your pediatrician.

Seek Help

If your child persists in having difficulty righting herself, it's important to seek professional help—even if you are using the exercises above to start dealing with this problem. Begin by contacting your baby's pediatrician, who may be able to determine if your infant's problem is caused by neurological impairment or a physiological difficulty. Remember to bring the records of your observations so that you can give a complete account of your child's motor development. Detailed records can be very helpful to a concerned physician.

If your baby's doctor doesn't respond satisfactorily to your concerns, don't hesitate to seek a second opinion. Chapter 9 will help you locate a physician or therapist who can evaluate your infant's development and provide the assistance she needs.

Righting—the action of rolling from a back-lying position to a stomach-down, all-fours position—can be seen as the gateway to motor independence. It enables the baby to crawl, to sit, and finally, to take her first steps. Just as important, it represents an essential step in a child's neurological development.

In most cases, righting begins at about four months of age, and quickly becomes part of the growing infant's repertoire of skills. But for some children—including many who are later diagnosed as being autistic or having Asperger's syndrome—righting is difficult to master, and sometimes is not mastered at all. Although these children usually find a way of getting from their back to their stomach, they often end up in a position that makes the transition to crawling difficult.

What of those children who *do* begin crawling? The next chapter examines this rung on the Ladder of Motor Development, looking both at normal crawling and at problems that some children encounter while trying to acquire this important skill.

CHAPTER 6

*C*rawling

Between six and ten months of age, the typical infant learns to crawl on hands and knees. Baby's first means of locomotion, crawling gives him complete freedom to move from one place to another on his own, without assistance from a parent or other caregiver.

This chapter starts by discussing the importance of crawling, and explains how it is performed by a nonautistic infant. It then describes crawling difficulties that may signal problems. Finally, it guides you in helping your child reach this motor milestone.

THE IMPORTANCE OF CRAWLING

As already mentioned, crawling is baby's first means of independently getting from one place to another. For this reason, crawling is important in and of itself, and is immensely satisfying to the child who craves independence. Just as important, like every other stage in motor development, crawling builds on past skills and makes possible the acquisition of future skills, such as standing and walking. As a child cruises along between pieces of furniture, he develops his muscles, coordinates right and left movements of legs and arms, fine-tunes his vision, and matures his reflexes. Crawling, therefore, is an important step in a child's overall physical and neurological development. In fact, some experts believe that children who skip crawling, and go straight to walking, miss an important developmental stage and are at increased risk for behavior disorders.

UNDERSTANDING THE NORMAL CRAWLING PROCESS

In Chapter 5, you learned how the infant masters righting—how he moves from a back-lying position to a stomach-lying position. Once he has attained that skill, he is prepared to make the transition to crawling. But first, he assumes what has been referred to as the *cat-sit position*—a position in which his legs are flexed (folded) under him; his arms are straight with his hands

Figure 6.1 The Symmetric Tonic Neck Reflex

A. When the infant's head is extended upward, this reflex causes the arms to straighten and the legs to bend in a cat-sit position.

B. When the infant's neck is bent downward, this reflex causes the arms to bend and the legs to straighten.

planted on the floor, supporting his chest; and his neck is extended, lifting his head forward in a vertical position. (See Figure 6.1A.) What enables him to get into this position is the *symmetric tonic neck reflex,* or *STNR.*

As first explained in Chapter 3, the symmetric tonic neck reflex is not present when an infant is born, but appears at four to six months of age. In a sense, this reflex divides the baby in two at the waist, making the upper and lower parts of his body work in opposite ways, controlled by the position of his neck and head. When the infant's neck is extended and his head lifts up, the arms extend, raising the upper half of his body and causing his legs to bend in the cat-sit position. (See Figure 6.1A.) When the infant's neck is bent downward, his arms bend and his legs straighten somewhat. (See Figure 6.1B.)

Before a baby begins to crawl, he may rock back and forth on his hands and knees, practicing shift of weight and coordination of limbs.

When you look at Figure 6.1, you can appreciate the see-saw nature of the STNR, which permits the baby to rock his weight back and forth. A shift of weight is necessary for all locomotion. Consider that when you walk, your two feet form the body's base. They make contact with the ground and carry your weight. To move forward, you must shift your weight from one side to another. Now consider crawling. Here, too, the weight must be shifted, but in this case it is more complicated because the body is supported by *four* bases—two legs and two arms. Once in the cat-sit position, the shift of weight back and forth can occur. Before taking their first crawling "step," many babies rock back and forth on their hands and knees, learning to shift their weight and coordinate the movement of their hands and legs. Both a smooth, continuous shift of weight and limb coordination are vital if the infant is to resist gravity and move forward.

You may already be aware that most babies try several means of loco-motion before they settle on the standard crawl. Some infants, for instance, first use *creeping*. In creeping, a baby's stomach touches the floor as he pulls himself along with his arms, with his legs dragging behind him. Many children use *inchworm crawling*, in which the infant's stomach is lift-ed off the ground, but again, his two arms work simultaneously to pull both legs forward. Some children move backwards at first. And some infants use a kind of bear walk in which—with their arms and legs straight and their bottom in the air—they "walk" on hands and feet. But between six and ten months of age, most children master what is known as the *contralateral crawl*, or *cross-crawl pattern*.

For the contralateral crawl, the baby must move from the cat-sit posi-tion to the crawling position by "walking" his hands forward until his

Many babies can be seen using creeping or inchworm crawling before they master true crawling. Some babies even move backwards before they move forwards. But the typical baby's efforts result in the contralateral crawl.

Figure 6.2 The Contralateral Crawl

A. The contralateral crawl starts with the baby's moving one arm forward.

B. After the baby's weight is shifted onto his first arm, the opposite knee is moved forward.

C. The crawling pattern is completed when the baby moves the second arm forward, followed by the second leg.

Although the symmetric tonic neck reflex, or STNR, makes it possible for a baby to begin crawling, this reflex must be suppressed if a child is to continue moving up the Ladder of Motor Development.

thighs and arms are vertical, and his trunk is horizontal and lifted off the floor. After he assumes this position, a baby starts the contralateral crawl by putting one arm forward. (See Figure 6.2A.) He then shifts his weight onto that arm, and steps forward with the opposite knee. (See Figure 6.2B.) Next, he walks his second arm forward, shifts his weight to that arm, and steps his second leg forward, completing the crawling pattern. (See Figure 6.2C.)

As we explained earlier, the STNR enables the baby to start crawling by getting him into the cat-sit position. But it's equally important to understand that as the baby practices crawling, his body is controlled less and less by this reflex. It is, in fact, essential that the reflex be suppressed, or "matured," if the baby is to crawl more efficiently. The more the infant crawls, the less he is under the grip of the STNR. Once he is free of this reflex—usually between eight to ten months of age—the infant can move his neck, arms, and legs independently of one another.

PROBLEM CRAWLING

After learning to right himself, the typical baby learns to crawl within a few weeks, and can soon be seen scooting across the floor, exploring his world. But as we've learned by examining videotapes, a number of infants later diagnosed as having autism or Asperger's syndrome show alternatives to the contralateral crawl.

By far, the most frequent atypical crawling pattern we've seen is *asymmetrical crawling.* In asymmetrical crawling, the contralateral crawl pattern remains. In other words, the baby first moves one arm forward and shifts his weight onto that hand. He then moves the opposite leg forward, followed by the second hand, and finally, the second leg. However, in this case, one side of the body does not mirror what the other side does. For instance, one leg may remain in the crawling position while the other leg assumes a walking position, with the lower leg vertical and the sole of the foot in contact with the floor. (See Figure 6.3.) This asymmetrical movement gives the baby's crawling a lopsided, limping quality, rather than the smoothness of the contralateral crawl. The pattern does not slow the baby down, though. Indeed, he seems to move around the room quite effectively.

Asymmetrical crawling is a clear example of persistent asymmetry, which was first discussed in Chapter 2. As you may remember, the two sides of an infant's body—left and right—typically develop in more or less the same way and at the same time, enabling him to move both sides equally. This symmetry can be seen in contralateral crawling. Both arms

**Figure 6.3
Asymmetrical Crawling**

In this form of asymmetrical crawling, one leg is held in the crawling position while the other leg assumes the walking position.

support the child's body, and the two legs are in a similar position and are able to crawl forward in the same manner. In asymmetrical crawling, the actions of the two legs are *not* mirror images of each other. While one leg is able to assume the proper crawling position, the other one is in a walking position. If you were able to spot persistent asymmetry in one of your baby's earlier motor development stages, it is likely that the same side will show an asymmetrical irregularity in crawling.

In another atypical crawling pattern, called *fall-over crawling,* the baby starts out on all fours, moves one arm forward, and follows with the opposite leg, as in typical contralateral crawling. (See Figure 6.4A.) But when he tries to complete the crawling cycle, he shifts his weight to the other arm without actually moving the arm to accept the weight. (See Figure 6.4B.) Without the support of the arm, the baby falls over. (See Figure 6.4C.) The naked eye may be unable to separate the components of fall-over crawling, but anyone can easily see that the baby consistently falls to one side when trying to crawl.

This second atypical crawling pattern can be described as a *gap of movement synergy.* Movement synergy is the harmonious coordination of the various motions involved in an activity. When a gap occurs in this synergy, there is inadequate synchronization between shift of weight and movement of limbs. The result is what is ordinarily called, for lack of a better word, clumsiness. Clumsiness is especially common in children who have Asperger's syndrome, although it can also be found in autistic children.

Even nonautistic babies may demonstrate asymmetrical crawling for a few "steps." But asymmetrical crawling does not persist in a typical baby.

Figure 6.4 Fall-Over Crawling

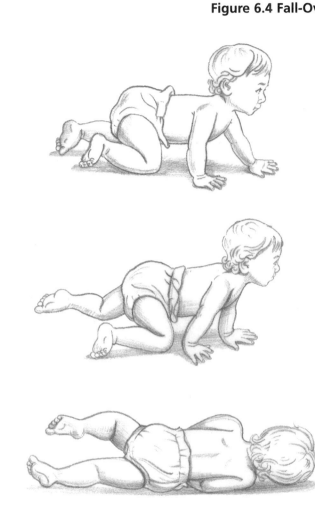

A. Fall-over crawling begins like typical crawling, with movement of the first arm and opposite leg.

B. The baby then shifts his weight to his second arm before the arm is moved to accept the weight.

C. Without the support of the second arm, the baby loses his balance and falls.

Both of the atypical movement patterns just discussed actually allow the baby to move from one place to another. But there are other atypical positions that do not permit the baby to crawl at all. In *rump-up crawling*, for instance, the baby leans forward on his arms as if to crawl. But instead of stepping forward with his hands and knees, the baby gets "stuck" with his rump raised in the air and his head on the floor. (See Figure 6.5.) Often, the baby who uses the rump-up position falls to the side when trying to crawl.

**Figure 6.5
Rump-Up Crawling**

In this form of atypical crawling, the baby gets stuck with his rump in the air, unable to move forward.

Another atypical pattern that causes the baby to become "stuck" occurs when the child assumes a knees-out sitting position rather than the knees-down position needed for locomotion. (See Figure 6.6.) In *sit crawling,* the infant tries to pull himself forward with his extended arms, but cannot move because his legs remain folded under him. This pattern may be an example of a disrupted reflex pattern. Fragments of the STNR remain in the form of folded legs, which may be an atypical form of the cat-sit position.

Last but not least, there are infants who skip crawling altogether. They pull themselves to standing, and at around ten months of age, they start to walk. Is this a problem? In some cases, children progress to walking without learning to crawl, and continue to develop normally without showing any symptoms of neurological impairment. However, in their book *Stopping ADHD,* authors Nancy O'Dell and Patricia Cook present compelling evidence that children who skip crawling miss an important

**Figure 6.6
Sit Crawling**

In this atypical pattern, the baby's legs remain folded under him as he tries to pull himself along with his arms.

Don't push your baby to speed through crawling and move on to walking. Crawling is not only a complicated process that requires practice, but also an important stage that is essential to proper development.

developmental stage, and may eventually acquire attention deficit and hyperactivity disorder (ADHD). Moreover, as you now know, if a baby skips the crawling stage altogether, he may fail to develop a mechanism that replaces the STNR. The reflex will then continue to appear long after the baby has completed his journey to independent walking, interfering with his motor and learning capabilities later in life.

WHAT YOU CAN DO

In most cases, within a few weeks of trying to master crawling, the typical baby succeeds in using the contralateral pattern. If your baby does *not* begin crawling by ten to twelve months of age, or if he persists in using an atypical pattern, it could be a cause for concern. For this reason, it is important to be aware of his progress.

Observe and Keep Records

As first explained in Chapter 2, no medical technology can replace a parent's careful observation of his child. You are in a unique position to see your baby move and change every day. You will know when he begins crawling, how he begins crawling, and if and when he masters the typical crawl that is so important to motor development.

As you observe your infant, keep a record of what you see, as explained on page 21. Your records can be in the form of a written diary or journal (see the Observation Journal on page 131), or in the form of a photo/video diary. These records will give you an accurate picture of what is happening with your child, and will also enable you to provide helpful information to your child's doctor and other professionals.

When observing your infant's crawling behavior, remember that contralateral crawling is a complicated process that takes practice before it can become a smooth, coordinated motion. Don't push your baby to speed up, but as the weeks pass, do look for certain signs that this developmental stage may not be progressing as it should.

- From the start, note whether the baby is showing any persistent asymmetry. Is he using one side of the body much more than the other? If so, is it always the same side, or does it differ from time to time? Does the asymmetry appear in only the upper body (the arms), or in the lower body (the legs) as well?

- Look specifically for any of the atypical crawling patterns described earlier in this chapter.

Encourage Crawling

If through your observations you have noted that your child appears to be struggling with crawling—or that he hasn't started crawling at all—here are some simple steps you can take to help your child meet this motor milestone.

- Encourage your child to crawl by providing ample opportunities for this activity. At least three or four times a day, position him stomach-down on a relatively firm surface, such as a carpeted floor. Make sure that he is comfortably warm and that his clothing allows for freedom of movement. Then lie down on the floor about six feet away and urge him to come to you, holding his favorite toy out in front of him. Remain in the room to provide support and to monitor his progress.

> Provide your baby with the time, the room, and the encouragement he needs to master crawling.

- Build an infant crawling track, as detailed in *How Smart Is Your Baby?* by Glenn and Janet Doman. (See page 125 of the Suggested Reading List.) This track, which you can construct in your home, is safe, clean, warm, smooth, and cushioned, providing your infant with maximum opportunity to move his arms and legs. The track is wide enough to enable the baby to easily move his legs and arms, but narrow enough to permit your child to push off the sides of the track with his feet.

- Do not place your infant in a walker. If your child is able to get around at will by using a walker, there's a chance that he will not be motivated to develop crawling skills.

- Do not overuse your child's playpen. This piece of equipment is a great place for your infant to safely play with his toys, but does not offer the space he needs to crawl. Make sure that several times a day, your infant has the opportunity to crawl over a large, flat, clean surface.

- Do not encourage your child to start walking early. Instead, give him the time he requires to learn and practice crawling. Remember that the process of crawling is not just a means of getting from one place to another, but also an important process that will prepare him for the mastery of more complicated skills. (For more information on the importance of crawling, see O'Dell and Cook's *Stopping ADHD*, listed in the Suggested Reading List on page 126.)

Seek Help

If your child is struggling with the task of crawling, and especially if he is showing one of the atypical patterns described in this chapter, it's important to seek professional help—even if you're working with your baby as just detailed. A good first contact is your baby's pediatrician, who may be able to determine if your child's struggle is being caused by a physical problem, such as hip dislocation, or is a possible symptom of neurological impairment. Remember to bring the records of your observations so that you can give a complete account of your child's motor development. Detailed records can be very helpful to a concerned physician.

If your baby's doctor doesn't respond satisfactorily to your concerns, don't hesitate to seek a second opinion. Chapter 9 will help you locate a physician or therapist who can evaluate your infant's development and provide the assistance he needs.

You now understand the importance of crawling as a rung in the Ladder of Motor Development. In addition to giving your baby new freedom, crawling matures reflexes, teaches the brain a complex action of coordination, and otherwise readies your child to reach future developmental milestones.

By the time a child is six to ten months of age, he is usually crawling well. But for some children, crawling does not develop in a typical manner, and may even signal the development of autism or Asperger's syndrome. This is why it's so important to be aware of your child's crawling progress and to take action when it is warranted.

Of course, the Ladder of Motor Development does not stop with crawling. The next chapter looks at another important milestone—sitting up.

CHAPTER 7

Sitting

When a newborn is held in a sitting position, her head droops forward towards her chest since she is not strong enough to resist gravity. A young infant simply does not have the balance needed to assume and maintain a sitting position. But within the first few months of life, both a child's strength and her balance begin to grow as she moves up the Ladder of Motor Development. And at around six months of age, she begins the process of learning to sit independently.

This chapter focuses on the process of sitting, which can be considered the halfway point in a child's early motor development—both chronologically and in a positional sense—as her upper half is vertical, but her lower half is still horizontal. The chapter first looks at the importance of sitting up, which, like other motor skills, is not only a great physical accomplishment, but also a steppingstone to further development and learning. It than examines the vestibular system, which plays a major role in providing the balance needed for sitting. It describes how a typical baby masters the process of sitting, and it explores the sitting difficulties encountered by some children later diagnosed as having autism or Asperger's syndrome. Finally, it explains what you can do to help your child develop this very important skill.

THE IMPORTANCE OF SITTING

Earlier chapters have explained that each rung on the Ladder of Motor Development is important because each skill boosts a child's physical development, enabling her to master further motor skills. For that reason alone, sitting is a significant achievement. As you will learn in this chapter, in order to sit upright without help, a baby has to develop her muscle strength, her coordination, and her sense of balance. All of these elements will be needed as a child progresses up the developmental ladder, learning to walk and run.

Sitting is important for another reason as well. When a baby can finally sit up without support, she has a new view of the world and a new freedom to use her arms and hands. She can stare at her hands and move them around, she can play with toys, and she can examine you and her immediate environment. All of these activities stimulate the higher centers of the brain, moving a baby closer to the mastery of talking, reading, writing, and many other pre-academic and academic skills.

THE VESTIBULAR SYSTEM

Located in the inner ear, the vestibular system monitors the body's motions and provides the feedback needed to maintain balance and orientation in space. Without this system, a child cannot sit, stand, or walk.

If you read Chapter 4, you may remember that the vestibular system is one of the three important systems of feedback that help the brain integrate and interpret sensory stimulation. The tactile system interprets information gleaned through touch; the proprioceptive system deals with information brought about by movement and muscular activity; and the vestibular system detects movement and changes in the position of the head, allowing the child to maintain balance and orientation in space. It is easy to understand why the vestibular system—one of the earliest sensory systems to develop in infancy—is so important in helping a baby move from a totally horizontal position to one in which the head and upper body are vertical.

The vestibular system actually monitors motion in two ways. First, through the semicircular canals, this system detects rotation (called *angular acceleration*), such as the movement that occurs when you nod or shake your head. Second, through structures called the utricle and saccule, the system detects motion along a line (called *linear acceleration*), such as the movement that occurs when an elevator drops beneath you or your body leans to one side. Let's take a look at the vestibular system and see how these structures work to keep tabs on the motion and position of your head.

The vestibular system is located on the inside of the skull, in each inner ear. (See Figure 7.1.) It is made up of three *semicircular canals*, which are positioned at right angles to one another so that each canal can detect motion on a single plane. Each canal is filled with a fluid call *endolymph,* and ends in a swelling called an *ampulla.* At its base, each ampulla holds sensory hair cells that project upwards into a gelatin-like mass called a *cupula.* When you turn your head in the plane of a canal, the endolymph fluid sloshes against the cupula, bending the hair cells and ultimately sending messages to the brain. The system is arranged so that when the canals on one side of the head are stimulated, the canals on the other side of the head are inhibited. This allows the body to keep track of the head's

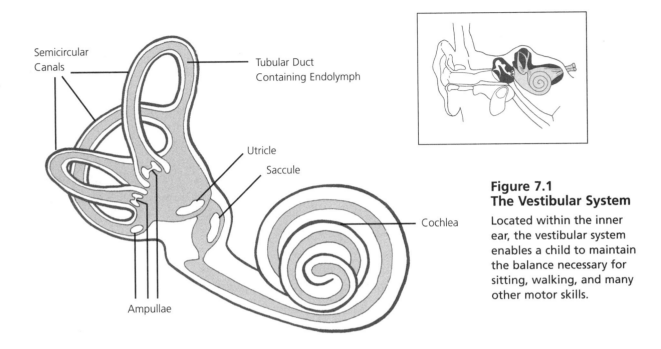

Semicircular
Canals

Tubular Duct
Containing Endolymph

Utricle

Saccule

Cochlea

Ampullae

Figure 7.1
The Vestibular System

Located within the inner
ear, the vestibular system
enables a child to maintain
the balance necessary for
sitting, walking, and many
other motor skills.

position without causing nausea or vertigo, which would result if both sides were activated at once. Note that a large role of the system of semicircular canals is to keep your eyes still in space while your head moves around. This is why you can maintain focus on this page even when nodding, shaking, or swiveling your head.

Each ampulla is connected to two membranous sacs, called the utricle and saccule. The *utricle* lays horizontally in the ear to detect sideways motion, while the *saccule* is positioned vertically to detect up-and-down motion. Each of these organs has a sheet of hair cells whose cilia are rooted in a gelatinous mass, similar to the arrangement found in the semicircular canals. When you move your head to one side, the gel bends the hair cells, and the brain is informed of the change in position. Note that a major role of the saccule and utricle is to keep you oriented vertically. When your head and body start to tilt, these structures enable you to compensate by making adjustments in your position.

As you can see, the semicircular canals, utricle, and saccule each perceive certain types of motions and transmit information about these motions to the brain, where it is interpreted. It is because of this system that you know the position of your head even in the dark, and can tell whether you are lying down, sitting or standing upright, leaning, falling, or turning.

UNDERSTANDING THE NORMAL PROCESS OF SITTING UP

Although parents can prop up a baby in a sitting position almost from day one, true independent sitting doesn't begin until a child is several months old and has developed the necessary sense of balance, muscular strength, and coordination. Let's take a look at the various stages a child goes through before she can sit up—and stay seated—by herself.

Between birth and about two months of age, if you hold a typical infant's wrists and gently pull her into a sitting position, her head hangs back limply. (By the way, it's not a good idea to hold her in this position for more than a moment or two.) But by about two months of age, when a child is pulled into a sitting position, she holds her head up in line with her body. Soon afterwards, she begins to use her abdominal muscles to actually *help* the person who's pulling her into the sitting position.

At about four months of age, a baby's head and neck muscles begin to strengthen more rapidly, and she starts to raise and hold her head up while lying on her stomach. At this point, when a baby sits on a parent's lap, she can probably hold her head steady for long periods of time and look around. Following this, she learns to prop herself up with her arms and hold her chest off the ground. Little by little, she is strengthening the muscles in her neck, her back, and her abdomen; developing her ability to coordinate the actions of different muscles; and maturing her vestibular system.

**Figure 7.2
A Typical Child
Sitting**

At about six months of age, the typical baby is strong and coordinated enough to sit without the support of parents or pillows.

Before a baby is able to sit truly independently, she usually learns to maintain a seated position by leaning forward with her arms out in front of her and her hands on the floor. Called *tripoding,* this allows an infant to sit up by herself before she has acquired the balance she needs to remain in a seated position unaided. Even with the help of her hands, though, a tripoding baby is likely to fall over to one side unless she is being kept stable through the use of pillows.

When a baby has developed sufficient stability and balance, she is finally able to sit with her hands resting in her lap, without any outside help. (See Figure 7.2.) At six to seven months of age—after the baby has mastered the righting process—she becomes strong and coordinated enough to move from a back-lying position to a sitting position, and then maintain that position.

PROBLEM SITTING

You now know how a typical baby progresses to the point where she can move from a lying-down to a sitting-up position, and then *stay* in that position without support from her own hands, pillows, or other people.

Unfortunately, our research has shown that some infants do not progress in the manner described earlier in the chapter.

We have found that a significant number of children later diagnosed with autism or Asperger's syndrome do not sit independently by six months of age. Many of the children who *are* able to sit, can't maintain the upright position, falling over much more often than normal children. Moreover, unlike typical children, these infants do not exhibit the *parachute reflex*—a reflex that usually appears before the onset of walking. When a normal child begins to fall, the parachute reflex causes her to extend her arms forward in an effort to protect her chest and head from hitting the floor, and to *slightly* tilt her head towards the vertical. (See Figure 7.3.) We have found that a child later diagnosed with autism or Asperger's syndrome keeps her arms and head in their original positions when falling, and as a result, may tumble onto her face. (See Figure 7.4.) She appears not to sense when she is toppling over.

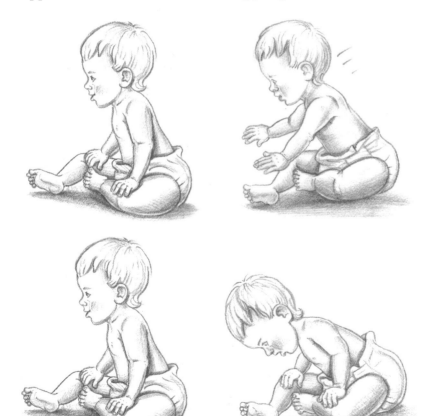

**Figure 7.3
A Child With a
Parachute Reflex**

When a typical child falls, she reflexively extends her arms in an effort to protect her head and chest.

**Figure 7.4
A Child Without a
Parachute Reflex**

When a child without a parachute reflex falls, her arms remain in their original position, offering her no protection.

The Teitelbaum Tilt Test

When a normal six-month-old infant is held in the air and *slowly* tilted about 45 degrees from the vertical, she responds by keeping her head vertical. (See the figures below.) This occurs—for a few seconds, at least—even when the baby's eyes are covered and she cannot use vision to determine her orientation in space. If you have read the rest of this chapter, you know that this indicates proper development of the infant's vestibular system.

In many cases, however, an infant who is later diagnosed as autistic does not show this ability. When tilted to the side, an autistic-to-be six-month-old infant tends to carry her head along passively with her body, so that both her body and her head end up at a 45-degree angle from the vertical. (See the figures on facing page.) This lack of head verticalization, which has been observed even in some seven-year-old autistic children, shows an impairment of the vestibular system, the body's system of balance.

The Teitelbaum Tilt Test (TTT) for autism is a good way to begin to determine if your child

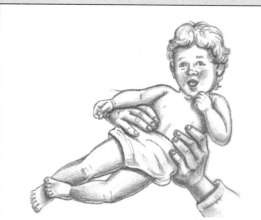 

A Typical Child Being Tilted to Her Left   **A Typical Child Being Tilted to Her Right**

Children with Asperger's syndrome and autism seem to have a problem with the vestibular system—the body's system of balance described on pages 70 to 71. This is supported not only by their lack of stability when seated and the absence of the parachute reflex, but also by the involuntary eye movement known as *post-rotatory nystagmus*. When a nonautistic child is spun around—in a revolving office chair, for example—her eyes repeatedly move slowly across the range of motion, and then reset quickly to the starting position. Autistic children do not demonstrate this pattern to the might be autistic. To use this simple test, *slowly* tilt your baby about 45 degrees to one side, at the same time noting whether she keeps her head vertical or allows it to tilt with the rest of her body. Then *slowly* bring your infant back to a vertical position and repeat the test on the other side, again observing your infant's response. Because some autistic children lack the ability to keep the head vertical on one side only, it is important to tilt your baby to both sides.

If you can, perform the TTT in front of a mirror. This can make it easier to see your child's response. It's also a good idea to record the TTT on a video camera. This not only will allow for closer and repeated examination of your infant's movements, but also will enable you to show your child's reaction to a pediatrician or other professional, if necessary.

Be aware that the TTT results are not meant to conclusively show that your child is or is not autistic. However, a lack of verticalization of the head does suggest neurological impairment, and should be brought to the attention of a professional. And when it appears along with other problem movement patterns described in this book, it may indicate autism or Asperger's syndrome.

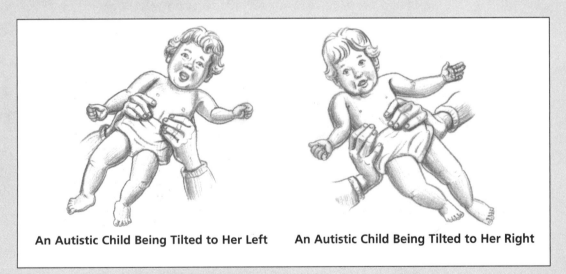

An Autistic Child Being Tilted to Her Left   **An Autistic Child Being Tilted to Her Right**

same degree that other children do. In fact, some children with autism show no nystagmus movements at all after spinning. Yet strangely, after a period of spinning, these children often do not feel dizzy and disoriented, as a typical child would.

Autistic children also often seek activities that can provide vestibular stimulation, such as amusement park rides that involve spinning around. This need for stimulation might also account for the stereotypical rocking pattern often seen in autistic children.

WHAT YOU CAN DO

When a child has trouble achieving and remaining in a stable seated position, an undeveloped vestibular system may be to blame.

As you've learned, by six to seven months of age, most infants are able to sit up without help, and remain in a stable seated position. But this does not occur with all children. If your child persists in having trouble sitting up and remaining upright, it could be a cause for concern. For this reason, it is important to be aware of her progress.

Observe and Keep Records

As first explained in Chapter 2, no technological marvel can replace a parent's careful observation of her child. You are in a unique position to see your baby move and change every day. You will know when she makes her first attempts to sit up, and if and when she masters the stable seated position that is so important to her future development.

As you observe your infant, keep a record of what you see, as explained on page 21. Your records can be in the form of a written diary or journal (see the Observation Journal on page 131), or in the form of a photo/video diary. These records will give you an accurate picture of what is happening with your child, and will also enable you to provide helpful information to your child's doctor and other professionals.

When observing your infant's efforts to sit, you are most likely to note problems if you focus on specific positions and movements, as explained below.

- When your child is around six months of age, test her ability to lift her head to a vertical position. When she is lying on her back, pull her up gently by her hands, and note if she makes an attempt to lift her head. If her head hangs down limply, it may be a cause for concern.

- When your child is six to eight months old, use the Teitelbaum Tilt Test for autism, explained in the inset on pages 74 to 75. This simple test can detect possible impairment of the vestibular system.

- If your baby is able to maintain her head in the vertical position, note if she attempts to raise her upper body, as well.

- If your child is able to reach a sitting position, note if she begins to assume the position more easily with continued practice.

- Note if your child is able to maintain a sitting position, or if she falls over repeatedly. If she does fall, observe the direction in which she falls—forward, backward, or to the left or right. Also notice if she shows the parachute reflex by extending her arms forward to protect her chest and head from hitting the floor.

Stimulate Your Baby's Sense of Balance

If through your observations you have noted that your child is unable to assume or maintain a sitting position, be assured there are ways in which you can help your baby develop the balance needed to sit.

- As long as the weather is nice, take your child to the park every day, position her on your lap in an adult-size swing, and swing back and forth. To keep your child secure, place her in a front-worn carrier so that she can't fall. To make your child *feel* secure, wrap your arms around both the ropes of the swing and her. (See Figure 7.5.)

  Continue the swinging until your baby wriggles to get off, thus signaling that she has had enough. Such a period of swinging may last as long as half an hour or forty-five minutes. During this time, the motion will stimulate the inner ear and help to regulate and develop balance. In one case, after three weeks of "swinging therapy," a three-month-old child not only showed improved balance, but also was more responsive to her mother. (See the inset below for more information on using this therapy.)

Figure 7.5
**Improving Balance
With a Playground Swing**

The simple back-and-forth motion of a swing can stimulate a child's vestibular system, helping develop her sense of balance.

Effectively Using Swing Therapy

As described above, you can help your child develop the balance she needs to sit by holding her on your lap in a full-size swing, and swinging back and forth. Weather permitting, this should be done every day for as long a period as your child will tolerate without wriggling to get off your lap. Over time, this simple activity can help your child's vestibular system to mature.

What if your child is scared by the motion of the swing? In that case, commence with a gentle motion and swing for a period of only a few minutes. Then each day, increase the range of motion and the time spent swinging. If even a gentle movement causes your child to scream

and cry, stop swinging. You should not do anything that frightens your child.

Would a small indoor infant swing provide the benefits of a full-size playground swing? Time spent in an infant swing may help your child's balance to some degree, but for best results, the more pronounced motion of the playground swing is needed.

Try to start your child's swinging therapy as early in her life as possible—even before she reaches the age when children begin to sit independently. The sooner you stimulate your baby's sense of balance, the more success she is likely to have in meeting motor milestones.

- As soon as your child is able to use other playground facilities, such as merry-go-rounds and slides, encourage her to do so. These, too, will stimulate your child's vestibular system.

Seek Help

If your child is struggling with the task of sitting or shows a poor response to the Teitelbaum Tilt Test (see page 74), it is important to seek professional help—even if you are using the tips above to start dealing with this problem. A good first contact is your baby's pediatrician, who may be able to determine if your infant's struggle is a possible sign of neurological impairment. Remember to bring the records of your observations so that you can give a complete account of your child's motor development. Detailed records are essential, as they enable you to effectively present your concerns to a physician or other professional.

If your baby's doctor doesn't respond satisfactorily to your concerns, don't hesitate to seek a second opinion. Chapter 9 will help you locate a physician or therapist who can evaluate your infant's development and provide the assistance she needs.

The world opens up to the baby who is able to sit up on her own, look around, and manipulate toys and other objects from her stable seat on the floor. With her improved coordination, muscle strength, and balance, this baby will soon be able to pull herself to a standing position. Then she will start the process of learning to walk—the subject of our next chapter.

CHAPTER 8

*W*alking

Throughout his first year of life, an infant gradually develops his motor skills as he moves towards standing upright and walking. Once he attempts his first steps, he has reached the zenith of the Ladder of Motor Development. Yes, he will learn how to run, ride a bicycle, and play ball. But all of these abilities depend on vertical posture.

This chapter first discusses the importance of walking, and describes how the typical child progresses from his first tentative steps to the smooth gait characteristic of mature walking. It then describes walking patterns often found in toddlers who were later diagnosed as having autism or Asperger's syndrome. Finally, it guides you in observing your child's progress and helping him reach this motor milestone.

THE IMPORTANCE OF WALKING

Like crawling, which was discussed in Chapter 6, walking is important in and of itself. Not only can baby now move at will, but he can do so in a manner that leaves his hands free to pick up, examine, and play with toys and other objects. The space he inhabits is enlarged as walking gives him access to new people and new objects of interest. By further raising his head up off the ground, walking gives the baby a different perspective, as well. No longer confined to seeing things from floor level, baby's view of the world changes considerably as a result of this new ability.

Of course, like all of the motor skills discussed in earlier chapters of the book, walking builds on previously acquired skills and makes possible the acquisition of future motor abilities. As a child walks independently, he develops his muscles, improves his coordination, and further enhances his sense of balance. At the same time, his interaction with new people and things stimulates all of his senses and helps mature his nervous system. Both the physical and neurological development that occurs as a result of walking is crucial if the child is to acquire new motor skills—running, skipping, jumping, throwing, and catching—as well as important language and perceptual skills.

UNDERSTANDING THE NORMAL WALKING PROCESS

When an infant starts to walk, his gait is composed of staccato movements, with long intervals of standing between steps. Only through practice can he achieve the smooth gait typical of adults.

Although the action that we call walking seems quite simple, it actually requires a high level of neurological organization and integration of sensory and motor mechanisms. That's why this ability can be acquired only after a child has spent months developing his muscle strength, his balance, and his coordination. Moreover, walking is typically mastered not all at once, but in stages, and demands a great deal of practice.

We are all familiar with the adult gait, which involves the relatively smooth and seamless shift of weight from one leg to the other. But when an infant starts to walk—usually, between eleven and thirteen months of age—his gait is very different. First, his feet point outward instead of straight ahead, because this provides him with a wider, more secure base of support. Second, unlike an adult, an infant cannot yet integrate the shift of weight with the stepping movement of the leg. Instead, these actions are separate and distinct from each other. Only after the baby establishes contact with the ground with his stepping foot is he able to shift his weight onto it.

The infant starts in a posture of stability in which he stands still, with both legs parallel and his weight evenly distributed. (See Figure 8.1A.) He then laterally shifts his weight to one leg, after which he lifts the other leg and steps it forward, moving it not directly in front of him, but diagonally out to the front and side. (See Figure B.) Because only the thigh is being actively moved, with the lower leg and foot being carried passively along, the step is very short. The foot is planted as a whole, with toes and heel touching the floor at the same time. (See Figure C.) Once the foot is in a stable position on the ground, the baby shifts his weight to the newly planted foot, releases the other leg from the ground (see Figure D), and moves it forward to a position parallel to the leg that first stepped. (See Figure E.) The movement of the second leg is performed quickly so that the infant can regain his balance, which is precarious at this point. The result is a "waddling" walk of staccato movements, with long intervals of standing between steps. For added balance, the infant's upper arms are raised to the height of his shoulders, parallel to the floor, and his forearms are held in a vertical position.

Figure 8.1
Early Infant Walking

A. The baby starts with his feet planted wide apart and his arms held high for better balance.

Front view   **Side view**

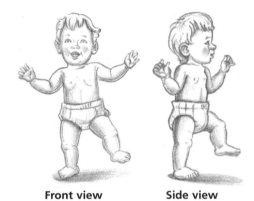

Front view   **Side view**

B. The baby moves his first leg forward and slightly to the side.

Front view   **Side view**

C. Because the baby does not extend his lower leg, each step is relatively short.

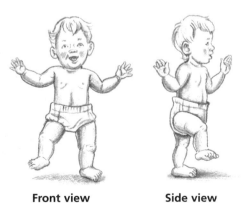

Front view   **Side view**

D. When the first foot is in a stable position, the baby moves his second leg.

Front view   **Side view**

E. When the baby completes his second step, the second leg is parallel to the first.

Figure 8.2 More Mature Infant Walking

A. The baby starts with feet planted a little closer together and arms a little lower—at about waist height.

B. The baby begins to move his first leg forward by raising his thigh. His leg is moved directly in front of him, not forward and to the side.

C. To complete the first step, the baby extends his lower leg before placing his foot on the ground.

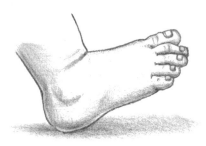

Figure 8.3
Baby's Foot Strikes
the Ground Heel First

At some point, the baby begins striking the ground heel first rather than planting the whole foot at once. This small change moves the child closer to a smooth, coordinated gait.

A short time after a baby begins to walk, he starts to recruit his lower leg in the walking process by extending that section of his leg after raising his thigh. (See Figure 8.2.) Although this makes the steps somewhat longer, he still places his foot flat on the ground as one unit. The arms are lowered to waist height, and the forearms are now parallel to the floor, rather than being vertical as they were when the baby first began to walk. At about the same time, the baby stops relying on such a wide base in the legs. He now places his stepping leg directly in front of him, rather than diagonally out to the front and side. At some point during this intermediate phase of walking, the baby reaches a turning point: When stepping forward, he strikes the ground with his heel first. (See Figure 8.3.) Although this change may seem trivial, it has far-reaching consequences. Once the baby's heel strikes the ground, the foot moves like a wheel, and the infant *rolls* his weight onto his foot as contact with the floor spreads from the heel towards the toes. When the baby becomes comfortable with this new mode of stepping,

D. Because the lower leg is now being recruited, the step is a little longer.

E. When the baby regains his balance, he moves his second leg.

F. Again, the baby extends his lower leg before placing his foot on the ground.

G. When the child completes his second step, his feet are parallel to each other.

he starts to transfer his weight forward *in anticipation* of the movement of his back foot. This is the beginning of a continuous shift of weight—the most distinctive property of a smooth, mature step.

Children enter the final phase of mature walking when just before the front heel strikes the ground, the rear heel lifts up, indicating that the weight is being shifted. (See Figure 8.4.) This small gesture enables a child to use a continuous motion while walking, rather than pausing ever so slightly in the center of the step to shift weight. Once the baby feels more securely balanced, he lowers his arms alongside his torso. It is at this point that he starts coordinating the movements of his arms with those of his legs. When stepping forward with the right leg, the left arm swings forward. When stepping forward with the left leg, the right arm swings forward.

Some babies speed through the process just described in a matter of a few days. Others take longer to learn to walk. And for some children, progress is made in fits and

Figure 8.4 Mature Infant Walking

When a child's gait matures, his rear heel lifts up slightly before his front heel hits the ground. His arms are lower and move in coordination with his steps.

Physical clumsiness is often associated with Asperger's syndrome. Asperger's children tend to be awkward and poorly coordinated, with a walk that can appear either stilted or bouncy. These kids usually have a history of developmental delays in gross motor skills such as catching a ball or climbing outdoor play equipment, as well as in fine motor skills such as brushing teeth, buttoning a shirt, or writing.

starts, with one day's advances being offset the next day, when the baby reverts to an earlier movement pattern.

Even typical children sometimes show asymmetry when they start to walk. For instance, a child may begin striking the floor heel first with one foot while continuing to move the other foot as a single unit. A child may also move his arms asymmetrically at various times. But in a typically developing baby, both reversions and asymmetries straighten themselves out in a matter of a few days, and the child soon develops a smooth, symmetrical gait.

If you read the previous chapter, you know how maturation of the vestibular system—the body's internal system of balance—is vital if a baby is to sit up by himself. It's easy to understand that this system is also important as a child learns to stand upright and walk. The proprioceptive system, which monitors motion and helps coordinate motor activity, as well as the tactile system, which enables the baby to feel the floor, are also key. (See page 43 for more information about these systems.) Once the baby masters standing and walking, the individual components of these actions are blended together so that walking becomes automatic, freeing the baby to more easily explore his environment.

**Figure 8.5
Persistent
Asymmetric
Walking**

In this form of persistent asymmetric walking, the child carries one arm low, as in mature walking, but holds the other one up in an infantile position.

PROBLEM WALKING

You are now familiar with the manner in which a typical baby progresses from a halting gait, composed of separate elements, to a gait that smoothly integrates the different components of walking. Although one child may start walking at a relatively young age while another child begins to walk a little later, by the time most kids reach their second birthday, their walk is fully integrated. Children later diagnosed as having autism or Asperger's syndrome, however, frequently have problems with the walking process. Some atypical gait patterns involve persistent asymmetry, a delay in the integration of the elements of mature walking, or a difficulty related to the vestibular system. Other problems common to autistic or Asperger's children have no known cause, but are very real nevertheless.

On page 83, you read that when learning how to walk, some children show an asymmetry for a short period of time. In other words, for a few days only, the two sides of the baby's body are not operating in the same way. Some autistic children, however, develop a *persistent asymmetry*—an asymmetry that lasts for a month or more. This can be easily recognized when one arm swings along as it should, moving forward as the opposite leg takes a step, while the other arm is held in a raised infantile position. (See Figure 8.5.) In our research, we have found autistic children who show this asymmetry even at eleven years of age. This clearly points to neurological damage.

Other autistic children show a primitive baby walk by failing to actively extend their lower legs. Thus, they strike the ground with their entire foot, rather than striking heel first. (See Figure 8.6.) As a result, they take much shorter steps than a normal child of the same age. This pattern has been seen even in autistic teenagers, demonstrating just how long a primitive walk can persist. Some parents have commented to us that their older child "walks just like a baby."

In children with autism or Asperger's, shift of weight, which is probably controlled by the vestibular system, is not always integrated with the movement of

**Figure 8.6
Primitive
Baby Walk**

In this form of atypical walking, the child walks like an infant by striking the ground with the entire foot.

the legs. For example, one five-year-old autistic child was seen to stand erect on one leg and perform a full-step movement of walking with the other leg *before* starting to shift his weight onto the stepping leg. (See Figure 8.7.) Because shift of weight was not integrated with the stepping motion, his stepping leg was straight in the air before he shifted his weight onto it. This pattern, which resembled a stiff-legged goose step, gave the impression that the child was falling onto his fully extended stepping leg. This is an example of a gap in movement synergy. First discussed in Chapter 6, *movement synergy* is the harmonious coordination of the separate movements involved in an activity. Gaps in synergy can be extreme, like the walking pattern just described, or can be the more subtle "clumsiness" exhibited when a child has problems kicking a ball in soccer, running in an athletic competition, or performing ballet.

Figure 8.7   Improper Shifting of Weight

A. As he begins to step his leg forward, the child fails to shift his weight onto the forward limb.

B. With the body's full weight still on the child's rear leg, the gait resembles a stiff-legged goose step.

C. When he finally transfers his weight forward, the child seems to fall onto his extended leg.

In addition to the three problems discussed above, each of which can be linked to a cause, two other walking problems are well-known phenomena among children with autism. The first problem is *toe walking,* in which the child walks high on the balls of the feet. The second is *hand flapping,* in which the child flaps his hands at shoulder height along the sides of his body while he walks. No cause is known for either of these behaviors, but both are more prevalent in autistic children than they are in typically developing children.

WHAT YOU CAN DO

As you've learned, by twelve months of age, most infants have begun taking their first steps, and by age two, they usually have mastered a smooth gait. But this does not occur with all children. If your older child persists in walking like an infant or shows any other problem behavior discussed in this chapter, it could be a cause for concern. For this reason, it is important to be aware of his progress and to record your observations.

Observe and Keep Records

As first explained in Chapter 2, no technological device can replace your careful observation of your child. You are in a unique position to see your baby move and change every day. You will know when he makes his first attempts to walk, and if and when he masters the mature gait that is so important to his future development.

As you observe your infant, keep records of what you see, as explained on page 21. Your records can be in the form of a written diary or journal (see the Observation Journal on page 131), or in the form of a photo/video diary—which is especially helpful when analyzing walking. These records will give you an accurate picture of what is happening with your child, and will also enable you to provide helpful information to your child's doctor and other professionals.

When observing your infant's efforts to walk, you are most likely to note problems if you focus on specific positions and movements, as explained below.

- Be aware that once your child starts to stand upright and walk, it might take him several weeks to integrate the various components of walking. But if he keeps falling even after a few months, it should be a cause for concern. When he falls, note whether he demonstrates the parachute reflex by extending his hands and arms to break his fall. (See page 73 for a discussion of the parachute reflex.) Also notice if he always falls to the same side.

  Never push your child to walk. But if your child begins to walk on his own and struggles to master the skill, make sure he gets the help he needs.

- Look for signs of persistent asymmetry, as described on page 84. For instance, when walking, does your child swing one arm while holding the other arm in a raised position?

- Watch to see if your child bends his legs properly while walking, or if he uses a stiff-legged goose-step gait.

- Note if your child has retained a primitive form of walking—a movement appropriate for a younger infant, but not for one who has been walking for months. For instance, does he still hit the ground with his entire foot rather than striking heel first?

- Note if your baby is persistently toe-walking—that is, standing high on the balls of his feet while walking. Many babies take their early steps on their toes, but this behavior should soon be replaced by a typical walking pattern.

Assist Your Child

We don't believe that you should push your child to walk before he demonstrates a desire to do so. Let him crawl on the floor as much as possible, as this will further his neurological and physical development, readying him for walking. If, however, your child has begun to walk on his own but continues to have problems after a month or two of trying, there are ways to help him.

- Avoid using a baby walker. This "shortcut" to walking can actually delay the learning process.

- Allow your child to walk barefoot both indoors and out, if possible. Our feet were created perfectly for walking, so there's no need for shoes while learning to walk. Moreover, direct contact of the foot against the floor stimulates nerve endings and use of the toes.

- If possible, instead of holding your baby's hands while he walks, kneel beside him and hold him by the torso. This will give him a sense of security without raising his hands unnaturally high in the air.

- Create a space in your house that will allow your child to practice walking without hurting himself when he falls. Every baby falls many times when learning to walk. By providing carpeted floors and eliminating furniture with sharp corners, you will allow your child to practice walking without fear.

- To improve your child's sense of balance, take him to the park every day, place him on your lap in an adult-size swing, and swing back and forth. (See page 77 for more information about improving development of the vestibular system through the use of swings.)

- If your child is six months of age or older, enroll him in an infant swimming class. Because there is no need to resist gravity during water activities, swim therapy can help improve a child's motor skills while building his self-confidence. Do *not* teach your baby swimming on your own. Instead, find a professional instructor who is experienced in working with babies.

Seek Help

If your child is struggling with the task of walking and shows one of the atypical walking patterns detailed in this chapter, it is important to seek professional help—even if you are using the tips above to start dealing with the problem. A good first contact is your baby's pediatrician, who may be able to determine if your infant's problem is caused by neurological impairment or a physiological difficulty. Remember to bring the records of your observations so that you can give a complete account of your child's motor development. Detailed records can be very helpful to a concerned physician or other professional.

If your baby's doctor doesn't respond satisfactorily to your concerns, don't hesitate to seek a second opinion. Chapter 9 will help you locate a physician or therapist who can evaluate your infant's development and provide the assistance he needs. A physical therapist who works with children in the first year of life would be an excellent choice.

A baby who is able to reach a stable standing position and achieve a smooth walk has risen to the peak of the Ladder of Motor Development. From this point on, he will continue to have many achievements, but all of them—including talking, reading, and writing—will be made possible by his mastery of these early motor skills. That is why it is so important to find appropriate help for a child who struggles to reach a rung on the ladder of development. The next chapter will guide you in your search for professionals who can properly diagnose your child's problem and provide the assistance he needs.

CHAPTER 9

Seeking Help

Since you have turned to this chapter, it is likely that through observation of your infant's motor skill development, you have found that she shows possible signs of autism or Asperger's syndrome. Throughout this book, we have suggested ways in which you can help your child overcome obstacles while climbing the Ladder of Motor Development. But professional help may be needed. This chapter is designed to guide you in finding the best assistance available for your child.

Before we look at individual options for your child, it's important to note that although a number of programs and therapies have been created to help children with autism, until now, it has not been possible to detect potential autism in children under two years of age. Therefore, you may run into problems when trying to enroll an infant or toddler in a program. Some free government programs may deny access to any child who has not received a definitive diagnosis of autism or Asperger's, and some doctors may be unwilling to provide such a diagnosis before a child is old enough to show language and socialization problems. Moreover, some therapists may be hesitant to work with a child who is so young.

Always remember that you are your child's best advocate. You may run into roadblocks, but with perseverance, you can find effective therapies. If you have greater financial resources, you may be able to avoid the paperwork and stringent requirements that are part of certain free programs. But even if you have sizeable resources, you must be a smart consumer when choosing help for your child. The Autism Society of America and many other groups—including those formed by concerned parents—may be able to guide you to the best therapies in your area, and steer you away from questionable programs. (See the Resources section on page 117.) In addition, when considering any treatment, it is vital for you to ask questions that will enable you to determine if that program or therapy would be of value to your child. (See the inset on page 92.)

This chapter first guides you in seeking a diagnosis for your child. It then reviews a number of potentially effective programs and therapies.

CONTACT YOUR PEDIATRICIAN OR A SPECIALIST

The usual doctor's appointment will not give you the time you need to discuss your child's development with her doctor. Ask for a consultation appointment of at least thirty minutes.

As mentioned in earlier chapters, a good initial step is to make an appointment with your pediatrician so that you can share what you've learned about your infant's development. Remember that it is vital to bring along any records you've kept of your child's movements, whether in written or videotape form. These records will give the doctor a more complete picture of your child's problem.

Because the typical appointment to diagnose a sore throat or earache is about ten minutes long, and will not give you a chance to sufficiently discuss the matter with the pediatrician, ask for a consultation appointment of at least thirty minutes. This will provide adequate time to express your concerns, present the record of your child's development, and allow the doctor to examine your infant. In preparation for the meeting, you may want to summarize your concerns in writing. This will supplement the records you've already made by gathering your thoughts, and can be a good means of starting the ball rolling. You don't want to write a long

---

Questions to Ask a Provider of Autism Treatment

If you are looking into treatments for your autistic child, you may wonder how you can evaluate the different programs and services available. The National Institute of Mental Health suggests that you ask the following questions of each treatment provider.

❏ How successful has the program been for other children?

❏ How many children have gone on to placement in a regular school, and how have they performed?

❏ Do staff members have training and experience in working with children with autism?

❏ How are activities planned and organized?

❏ Are there predictable daily routines?

❏ How much individual attention does each child receive?

❏ How is progress measured? Is each child's behavior closely observed and recorded by the staff?

❏ Is each child given tasks and rewards that are personally motivating?

❏ Is the environment designed to minimize distractions?

❏ Does the program prepare parents to continue the therapy at home?

❏ What are the costs, time commitment, and location of the program?

essay, but to express the major points you want to make in a concise form. A numbered list will be fine.

Remember that you're not asking your pediatrician to diagnose autism, because that is beyond the range of most primary care providers. However, among other things, he may be able to identify (or rule out) physiological disorders that can masquerade as neurological impairment. While some autistic children appear to be deaf because they tune out the sounds around them, some infants actually *are* hard of hearing. Similarly, a child may have poor eyesight or a disorder of the arm, leg, or foot that can cause her to have trouble with certain motor skills. Although an observant parent can determine that there is a problem, a qualified professional is needed to administer the tests that can pinpoint the precise cause of the problem. It is often a mistake to make a diagnosis—or rule out a diagnosis—on your own.

Whether your doctor feels that your child may have autism or is more likely to have a problem such as poor eyesight, he should refer you to a specialist who can perform the necessary evaluation. Depending on the pediatrician's assessment, he may, for instance, send you to an expert in infant neurology, audiology, or ophthalmology. He may also refer you to a *developmental behavioral pediatrician,* who is trained in the assessment and treatment of children with developmental delays, developmental disabilities, and chronic conditions that can affect a child's learning and behavior.

It would be misleading to say that every pediatrician will take you seriously when you approach him with concerns about your child's motor development or behavior. Some pediatricians are likely to be quite sympathetic and helpful. Many pediatricians, however, may not be aware of the relationship between motor development, autism, and Asperger's syndrome. When faced with a child who is righting herself in an atypical manner, your baby's doctor may merely assure you that things will work out in time. It is true that when first learning a new motor skill, many children go through a period of trial and error during which they use unusual ways to complete the task. But if a problem movement pattern persists for a few weeks, and especially if it appears in combination with other atypical patterns discussed in this book, you should actively seek out a specialist or program that will give your child the attention that she needs and deserves.

Every child goes through a period of trial and error when learning a new motor skill. But if an atypical movement pattern persists for several weeks, it's important to find a professional or program that can help your child.

FIND TREATMENT FOR YOUR CHILD

If your child has been diagnosed as having autism or Asperger's syndrome, or if you strongly suspect that she has one of these conditions, rest

Where Can You Find the Help Your Child Needs?

Throughout this chapter, we mention agencies and organizations that offer programs for autistic children, can guide you to these programs, or can put you in touch with professionals who may be of assistance to your child. Contact information for these programs and organizations can be found in the Resources section, which begins on page 117.

Don't overlook the help available through the Autism Society of America (ASA). Your local ASA chapter can assist you in finding medical professionals, treatment centers, and other facilities in your area.

Finally, when searching for qualified physical therapists, occupational therapists, and other medical assistance, try contacting your local teaching or children's hospital. In addition to putting you in touch with medical professionals, these hospitals sometimes offer special programs for children with autism.

Each child with an Autism Spectrum Disorder is unique, with her own strengths and weaknesses. That's why there is no such thing as a one-size-fits-all therapy for autism. Moreover, as your child grows and changes, her treatment will have to be tailored to her needs.

assured that there are many therapies that can help your infant learn necessary skills and overcome a variety of developmental disorders. From free government services to school-based therapies and in-home treatments, assistance is available. With the right treatment, as well as love and support from you, your child can learn, grow, and flourish.

Now that you have become aware of your child's motor skill problems, timely action is crucial. Whether your baby has autism or another developmental delay, the very best thing you can do is get her appropriate treatment right away. *Don't wait to see if your infant will "catch up," and don't wait for an official diagnosis.* Early intervention will give you the best possible chance of enhancing your infant's development and reducing the symptoms of autism.

The following discussions will guide you in finding therapies for children with autism and other developmental disorders. We will first look at programs that directly work with autistic children or that teach parents how to provide home-based therapy. We will then look at the option of putting together individual therapies by assembling a team of specialists. Just remember that these two possibilities—a set program and individually selected therapies—are not mutually exclusive. You can, for instance, enroll your infant in a local program for autistic children, and arrange for at-home physical therapy as well.

Enroll Your Child—or Yourself—in a Program

A variety of programs are available for autistic children. Some offer professional care and therapy in your home; some offer professional treatment in a special facility; and some provide you, the parent, with the knowledge and instruction you need to work with your child.

Applied Behavior Analysis (ABA) Programs

Applied Behavior Analysis, or ABA, is based on the theory that behavior which is rewarded is more likely to be repeated than behavior which is ignored. During the early 1960s, behavior analysts began working with young children with autism and related disorders. Since then, a large number of ABA techniques have been developed to build useful skills and behaviors, ranging from motor skills to communication skills to reading and writing. ABA is also used to eliminate problem behavior such as twirling, finger-flicking, and rocking.

In a well-designed ABA program, children usually work on a one-on-one basis with a trained ABA professional, anywhere from twenty-five to forty hours a week. When a task is completed successfully, a reward is given, reinforcing that particular behavior. For instance, if the professional's goal is to increase eye contact, this behavior may be prompted either physically or verbally. The child is then given a reward such as a piece of candy. Problem behavior is not rewarded.

Critics of ABA say that it is too structured, and that the kids become too reliant on the prompts. They also believe that the skills taught in ABA are not generalized to apply to other aspects of the child's life. However, in recent years, behavioral therapists have tried to address these concerns by working with children in less clinical settings.

Because of the large demand for Applied Behavior Analysis for autism, a great many individuals and programs claim to offer ABA. It's important to find a program that is designed and supervised by a qualified behavior analyst who has had extensive experience in providing treatment for autistic children. (See the inset on page 92 for other tips on choosing a treatment provider.) Keep in mind, too, that current ABA requires a child's active participation, so at this time, ABA is designed for kids who are at least two and a half years of age.

To learn more about Applied Behavior Analysis, visit the website of the Cambridge Center for Behavioral Studies. (See page 119 of the Resources section.) In addition to providing information about ABA and autism, this website offers guidelines for selecting qualified behavior analysts.

Easter Seals Disability Services

All across the country, Easter Seals programs provide a wide variety of services for children with all types of disabilities, including autism. In most cases, this assistance is offered free of charge through state programs.

> Applied Behavior Analysis, or ABA, helps autistic children build useful skills and behaviors. Just be sure that the program you choose is designed and supervised by a qualified behavior analyst who has worked extensively with autistic children.

In nearly every state, Easter Seals offers special early intervention services for young children—including infants—with autism. These services may include physical therapy that helps an infant learn early motor skills, occupational therapy that allows a child to hold her own bottle, speech therapy, and more. Treatments are sometimes provided in the home, and sometimes offered in local child-care facilities. In addition, Easter Seals Child Development Centers provide child care for kids of all ages and abilities. About 25 percent of the children who attend these centers have disabilities such as autism.

To learn more about the services provided by Easter Seals in your area, visit the Easter Seals website or contact the organization by phone. (See page 119 of the Resources section.)

Floortime

Floortime has the distinction of being appropriate even for very young children. This child-friendly approach can be used by either a trained therapist or a parent.

Developed by Dr. Stanley Greenspan, Floortime is a form of therapeutic play in which an adult literally joins a child on the floor in an activity that interests her. The adult then initiates communication with the child about that activity, with the goal of building important skills. This approach, which is appropriate even for very young children, can be used by either a trained therapist or a parent. Critics of Floortime say that insufficient research has been performed to support the therapy's effectiveness, but proponents view Floortime as a warm approach that is able to reach autistic children.

Information on Floortime, including a database of certified clinicians, can be found on the Floortime Foundation's website. (See page 120 of the Resources section.)

Free Government Services

Under the federal law called the Individuals with Disabilities Education Act (IDEA), all children with disabilities, including those with autism, are eligible for a variety of free or low-cost services. Children in need, as well as their families, can receive medical evaluations, physical therapy, speech therapy, assistive technology devices, psychological services, parent counseling and training, and other specialized services. Be aware that technically, children under ten years of age do not need a diagnosis of autism to receive free services under the IDEA. If they are experiencing a developmental problem, they are eligible for early intervention and special education programs.

The government services for autistic children are geared to the age of the child. Infants from birth to the age of two are eligible for the Early Intervention Program. A free evaluation is provided to determine if your child qualifies for this service. If a developmental problem is revealed, early intervention treatment providers will work with you to create an Individualized Family Service Plan (IFSP), which explains your child's needs and the services she will receive.

Children of three years of age and older are eligible for special education services—school-based programs, in other words. Like the Early Intervention Program, this program is tailored to the needs of each child through an Individualized Education Plan (IEP). Autistic children are often placed in small groups with other developmentally delayed children so that they can receive specialized attention and instruction. Depending on their abilities, they may also spend part of the school day in a regular classroom.

As first mentioned on page 96, although these services are ostensibly available to every child who needs them, *in practice,* it is not always possible to obtain government help. Sometimes assistance is denied if a child has not received an official diagnosis of autism. In other cases, the existing services may not be geared for children under two years of age. Don't be surprised if you encounter roadblocks when applying for these programs.

If you are interested in locating early intervention services for your child, you can ask your pediatrician for a referral or contact the National Early Childhood Technical Assistance Center (NECTAC). (See page 120 of the Resources section.) If you want to learn about special education services, your local school system will be able to help you.

> Under the Individuals with Disabilities Education Act, free and low-cost services are available to all disabled children—even infants. Be aware, though, that you may encounter obstacles when trying to access this government-provided assistance.

The Institutes for the Achievement of Human Potential

Located in Philadelphia, Pennsylvania, The Institutes for the Achievement of Human Potential is a nonprofit educational organization that was founded in 1955 by Glenn Doman, a pioneer in the field of child brain development. The Institutes offers a comprehensive program for brain-damaged children, including autistic children, that focuses on a child's neurological growth and development.

What Is Assistive Technology?

In reading about the available treatments and therapies for autistic children, you may come across the mention of *assistive technology.* This term refers to any equipment or item—whether low-tech or high-tech—that can help an autistic child or adult function better. Commonly employed in physical, speech, and occupational therapy, assistive technology may include picture cards, dry erase boards, and photo albums that promote nonverbal communication; computers that are controlled by a special touch screen; games that enhance specific skills; or even weighted vests that discourage *stimming*—self-stimulating activities such as rocking.

The Institutes for the Achievement of Human Potential has been working with brain-injured children for over half a century. Once the Institutes determines which areas of the brain are hurt, it provides parents with a six-month program to use with their child at home.

The Institutes holds the view that autism is not a diagnosis, but a description of one symptom of a brain-injured child. It emphasizes the need to determine which areas of the brain are hurt as well as the extent to which they are injured. Once this is determined, The Institutes works with parents to provide them with the knowledge they need to help their child towards wellness. Lectures, demonstrations, and practical instruction are provided. Finally, based on the nature of the child's brain injury, parents are given a six-month program to use with their child at home. Every six months, parents return to The Institutes, where the child is re-evaluated and a new six-month program is created. By putting The Institutes' methods to work, parents can often train the infant's uninjured portions of the brain to do the work of the injured portions, and can thus help their baby learn crawling, walking, and other motor skills; can teach their child language skills; and can otherwise promote healthy neurological, physical, and emotional development.

To learn more about The Institutes for the Achievement of Human Potential, visit The Institutes' website or contact the organization by phone. (See page 122 of the Resources section.)

Kris' Camp

Kris' Camp is a nonprofit organization established in 1995 for children with autism and autism-like challenges. With camps in Arizona, California, and Connecticut, the program provides multidisciplinary therapy through physical, speech, occupational, art, and music therapists. The camp also offers respite and support for the parents and siblings of special children. The week-long program is tailored to meet individual needs and to maximize independence and self-esteem.

To learn more about Kris' Camp, visit the camp's website. (See page 119 of the Resources section.)

Neurologic Music Therapy Services of Arizona

The Neurologic Music Therapy Services of Arizona (NMTSA) provides rehabilitative music therapy for people with autism and other neurologic and developmental disabilities. *Not* a listening program, NMTSA involves the disabled person in actual music-making to treat cognitive, sensory, and motor dysfunction through rhythm. NMTSA provides on-site therapy for children living in the Phoenix area, and offers parent training for out-of-state families who want to work with their child at home. Infants as young as eight months of age have benefited from this program.

To learn more about NMTSA, visit their website or contact them by phone. (See page 121 of the Resources section.)

Relationship Development Intervention

Created by Dr. Steven Gutstein, Relationship Development Intervention, or RDI, appears to be a mix of ABA and Floortime, and also pulls activities from sensory integration therapy. (See page 102 for information on sensory integration therapy.) Through workshops and seminars, parents are helped to determine realistic, achievable goals. The staff then constructs a program tailored to the family's specific needs, and provides parents with one-on-one training in effective coaching so that they can work with their child. While critics say that research on this therapy is lacking, proponents believe that RDI is a clear, systematic approach designed to address the core issues of children with autism.

To learn more about Relationship Development Intervention, visit the RDI website or contact their Connections Center by phone. (See page 123 of the Resources section.)

The Son-Rise Program

Offered by the Autism Treatment Center of America, the Son-Rise Program was created by Barry and Samahria Kaufman, who successfully worked with their own severely autistic son, bringing him to full recovery. Designed for the parents of children who are challenged by autism, Asperger's syndrome, and other developmental difficulties, the Son-Rise Program teaches parents how to play with their child in a way that promotes emotional growth, socialization, and skill acquisition. Parents are encouraged to join the child in her favorite activities, thereby creating a respectful, trusting, interactive bond. The Start-Up Program offers five days of group training for parents who want to work towards their child's recovery. Families that need further help can attend more intensive programs that involve the child as well as the parent.

The Son-Rise Program was created by Barry and Samahria Kaufman when their own son, Raun, was diagnosed as severely and incurably autistic. Since then, the Kaufmans have taught their home-based program to other parents of autistic children.

To learn more about the Son-Rise Program, visit the website of the Autism Treatment Center of America. (See page 122 of the Resources section.)

Put Together a Team of Specialists, Therapies, and Activities

Many parents choose to gather their own team of hand-picked therapies and activities, geared for their child's needs. On the following pages, you'll find a list of available treatments that you may want to consider. Be aware that the appropriateness of various therapies depends not only on a child's strengths and weaknesses, but also on her age. For instance, while physical and occupational therapy are useful for even a six-month-old-child—and are the *best* means of helping an infant with poor motor skills—medication is not appropriate until a child is older.

Auditory Integration Training

Auditory Integration Training is just one type of aural therapy available for autistic children. Others include the Tomatis Method (see page 103) and rehabilitative music therapy (see page 98).

Developed by Guy Berard, a French doctor, auditory integration training (AIT) was designed to help people with autism, dyslexia, hyperactivity, and a range of other behavioral and learning disorders. Individuals with these problems often have hearing that is disorganized, asymmetrical, hypersensitive, or otherwise distorted. AIT addresses these problems through the use of musical programs that are modified by filtering certain frequencies of sound. While critics point to the lack of scientific evidence for AIT's efficacy, proponents cite the prevalence of auditory sensitivity in people with autism and Asperger's syndrome.

To learn more about AIT and to locate practitioners in your area, visit the Berard AIT Website. (See page 121 of the Resources section.)

Facilitated Communication

Facilitated communication is a strategy used by people without functional speech. A communication partner, or facilitator, helps the disabled individual use a communication device—a picture board, speech synthesizer, or keyboard—through physical contact. This contact may simply provide the disabled person with stability in a seated position, or may actually support the person's hand as it uses the communication device.

Facilitated communication has both its detractors and its supporters. Detractors point out that facilitators can easily influence the disabled individual, and thereby control her communication. Supporters recognize that over time, some people with autism have learned to communicate independently, without the help of a facilitator.

To learn more about facilitated communication, visit the website of the Facilitated Communication Institute of Syracuse University. (See page 120 of the Resources section.)

Medication

Although no medication can "cure" autism, some drugs have been used successfully to deal with autism-related problems such as hyperactivity, anxiety, and aggression. Once these symptoms have been minimized, the individual can often focus and learn with greater ease. The drugs used to treat the symptoms of autism include antidepressants such as Prozac, antipsychotics like Haldol, hyperactivity drugs such as Ritalin, and many more.

It is our opinion that these medications should never be given to infants or even to young children. Later in life, however, appropriate medication can be an important part of treatment. When your child is older, you may want to discuss this possibility with her doctor.

Nutritional Therapy

Although this is a controversial area, many parents believe that dietary interventions have helped their autistic children. Moreover, many autistic children have gastrointestinal problems that may benefit from dietary changes or the use of supplements. For these reasons, you may want to implement a diet that eliminates gluten (wheat and other grains) and casein (dairy)—the two main dietary culprits identified in the war against autism. If you have a young baby who screams after being fed her usual formula, a predigested formula may be helpful.

If you are interested in learning more about nutritional therapy for autism, visit the website of the Autism Network for Dietary Intervention. (See page 122 of the Resources section.) There, you will find articles on nutrition, answers to frequently asked questions, a list of professionals and practitioners, and a parent support system. It should go without saying that no nutritional changes should be made without consulting with your child's doctor.

Many parents believe that dietary changes have helped their autistic child. Most commonly, the child's diet is modified through the elimination of gluten (a protein found in wheat, barley, oats, and rye) and casein (a protein found in dairy products such as milk and cheese).

Occupational Therapy

Years ago, an occupational therapist (OT) might have worked with an autistic child to help her develop skills like writing, buttoning a shirt, tying shoes, etc. But OTs who specialize in autism now work not only on developing the practical skills needed for everyday life, but also on play skills and social skills, and on enhancing sensory integration. As a child grows, an OT can also devise strategies to help her make the transition from one setting to another—from home to school, for instance—and from one life phase to another.

If you'd like to find an occupational therapist for your infant, start by asking your child's pediatrician for a referral. In addition to offering the name of a qualified OT, your child's doctor can provide a prescription that will allow your therapist to bill her hours to medical insurance. Local children's and teaching hospitals can also put you in touch with a capable OT.

Although people commonly think that occupational therapists work only on developing the practical skills needed for everyday life, OTs also help improve social skills, and can even provide sensory integration therapy (see page 102).

Physical Therapy

Physical therapy is one of the best means of helping an infant who has poor motor skills. Moreover, this therapy is often covered by insurance.

If your child is very young, a physical therapist (PT) can help her learn basic motor skills such as sitting independently, righting, standing, and walking. As your child grows, the therapist can work on more advanced skills such as throwing, catching, and kicking a ball, as well as on general posture, balance, coordination, and strength. In most cases, the PT will work not just with your child but also with you so that you can continue the therapy at home for maximum effectiveness.

Like occupational therapists, physical therapists can often be found through your child's pediatrician or by contacting local children's and teaching hospitals. If these routes don't lead you to a good therapist, try the American Physical Therapy Association (AMPTA). (See page 122 of the Resources section for contact information.) Like occupational therapy, physical therapy is often covered by insurance.

Sensory Integration Therapy

Sensory integration dysfunction—the inability to accurately process sensations—is a hallmark of autism. As you learned in earlier chapters, autistic children may be overly sensitive to sounds, touch, movements, and sights; underreact to sensory stimulation, and therefore seek out intense sensory experiences; have coordination problems; and show other signs of this dysfunction. Sensory integration therapy teaches the nervous system to process stimuli in a normal fashion, thereby improving concentration, physical balance, motor skills, and impulse control. While critics say that the effectiveness of sensory integration lacks research support, proponents point out that many people with autism have difficulty in processing sensory information.

Sensory integration therapy is usually performed by a physical or occupational therapist, and is often covered by insurance. (See earlier discussions on locating these professionals.)

Speech and Language Therapy

When your child is old enough to acquire speech, a speech therapist can improve her verbal skills and language ability. A therapist can also enhance the nonverbal communication and social skills that autistic children must acquire in order to get along with others. In other words, in addition to learning how to say "good night," your child may be taught when, how, and to whom this should be said, and may also work on conversation strategies. This therapy is appropriate when a child reaches about two years of age.

Schools and early intervention providers usually provide speech and language therapy free of charge. If you wish to find a qualified speech therapist on your own, you can ask for a referral from your child's physician, contact your local children's or teaching hospital, or get in touch with the American Speech-Language-Hearing Association (ASHA). (See page 123 of the Resources section.)

Swim Therapy

Because there is no need to resist gravity during water activities, swim therapy can help improve a child's motor skills while building her self-confidence. At this time, there are no swimming classes geared especially for autistic children. However, there are infant swimming classes that work with babies six months of age and older. Do *not* teach your baby swimming on your own. Instead, find a professional instructor who is experienced in working with infants. Classes offered by Swim America or your local YMCA would be a good starting point. (See page 123 of the Resources section.)

Do *not* try to teach your baby how to swim on your own. Instead, find an instructor who is experienced in working with infants. Your local YMCA is a great place to start the search.

The Tomatis Method

Developed by French physician Alfred A. Tomatis, this listening therapy is based on the link between the ear, the voice, and the brain. By stimulating the auditory system with sounds of different frequencies, the Tomatis Method has been reported to decrease hypersensitivity to sound, improve language skills, increase social skills, enhance eye contact, and result in less aggressive behavior in children with autism. Although research has not been performed to support use of this method, anecdotal evidence shows it to be an effective means of reducing the symptoms of autism.

If you are interested in exploring this therapy, you can contact either the Spectrum Center or Integrated Listening Systems. The Spectrum Center offers a therapeutic application of sensory stimulation programs, with the Tomatis Method as its cornerstone. It can treat children at its facility, and can also enable parents to treat their children at home by providing them with the necessary equipment and instruction. Integrated Listening Systems (ILS) produces listening-therapy equipment based on the Tomatis Method. Although ILS does not provide Tomatis Method therapy directly to children with autism, its website offers a list of ILS practitioners. (See page 121 of the Resources section for contact information.)

Once treatment has begun, always remember that parental involvement is necessary to success. You can optimize your child's success by working with the people on your treatment team and following through at home whenever possible.

LIFE WILL CHANGE

Certainly, parenting is never easy, and raising a child with special needs presents even greater challenges. Regardless of the type of treatment you find for your child, it will take time and energy for you to care for her, and life will change as you work with your child and become involved in her care and development. While great victories and achievements lie ahead, there may be days when you feel discouraged and overwhelmed. That's why it's so important for you to take care of yourself.

Fortunately, there are many places that you can turn to for advice, advocacy, and support. You can even find respite care—temporary care provided for your child so that you can have a break. The Autism Society of America can help you find parent support groups in your area, and also offers a good deal of useful information and advice. The Respite Locator Service can guide you to local respite care tailored to your needs. (See the Resources section for information on these groups.)

If you find that anxiety or depression are beginning to interfere with your ability to function, you may also want to consider individual, marital, or family counseling. Therapy can give you the opportunity to talk honestly about your problems and express how you're feeling. Marriage and family counseling can help you and other members of your family cope with the challenges of life with an autistic child.

Help is available for your autistic infant, and for you and the rest of your family, as well. It may take some time to find the program or combination of therapies that work best for your child, but when the right treatments are provided as early in life as possible, great progress can be made.

*C*onclusion

This book is the result of two decades of work and effort. For most of that time, as researchers, we have sought to share our findings in academic peer-reviewed journals. While our articles have certainly reached a segment of the scientific community, we think it is time to write to a broader audience. Although we have tried to touch on all aspects of autism within these pages, our research has always focused on the early detection of autism and Asperger's syndrome. We know that in many regards, our work is radically different from that of others in the field. Instead of relying on language deficits and socialization to identify autism, we rely on an infant's physical movements, which can signal a problem long before a child acquires language and begins to take part in social activities.

We believe that this book is an important first step towards preventing or lessening the devastating effects of autism and Asperger's. Our goal is to provide you, the parent, with the tools you need to turn your "intuition" about your child—the sense that something is wrong—into knowledge and positive action. Don't be surprised if you encounter skepticism on the part of physicians and other professionals when you express concerns about your child's motor development. It takes time for any new approach to be fully understood and accepted. Remember that you are your child's most important advocate. By learning as much as you can and sharing that knowledge with other parents, with autism organizations, and with professionals involved in infant care, you can make a profound difference not only in the life of your own child, but in the lives of children around the world.

You are probably aware that there is now an explosion of information about autism, its causes, and its treatment. With this explosion has come a range of controversies. For instance, during the last few years, the incidence of autism among children has greatly increased. While some believe that this condition has become more common, others attribute the rise of cases to a broader definition of autism that includes more behaviors and, therefore, more children. The truth is that if your child has autism, you don't care about statistics or the controversy surrounding them. You care only about helping your child.

One of the many topics under debate involves the role of vaccinations in the development of autism. Some parents still attribute new cases of the disorder to thimerosal, a mercury-containing preservative that was long used in infant vaccines. The fact is that thimerosal is no longer found in any vaccines used before the age of seven. Nevertheless, some parents feel that a hazard is posed by combination vaccines, such as the measles-mumps-rubella vaccine (MMR) that is often administered when a child is around eighteen months of age. If you are concerned about the potentially harmful effects of vaccinations, but still want to provide your child with protection from disease, we suggest a commonsense approach. Have your pediatrician administer these three vaccines separately, rather than in combination, and insist that he space them out and begin them a little later in your child's life. If your baby starts receiving vaccinations when he is two years of age, and the separate components are provided at spaced intervals of at least a month or two, your child's system will be more mature and better able to handle the shots, and he will get the protection he needs without having to endure a heavy barrage of vaccines.

Perhaps the most controversial topic in the field of autism is that of treatment. While one person will report the great effectiveness of a given therapy, another person will condemn that same therapy as being useless. Because the focus of our work has always been on detection, the treatment recommendations we make in this book are based on the autism professionals with whom we have shared our research. Unfortunately, there is no magic bullet that will equally help every child with autism. As your child's advocate, and as the person who probably best knows his strengths and weaknesses, you may have to examine and try several treatments before finding the therapy (or therapies) that is most helpful.

As both scientists and parents, we have considered if the material presented in this book will give rise to false concern among parents of young children. Certainly, our intention is not to scare parents. We believe that it is time to bring our findings to the public, and we feel confident that as additional data comes in, the link between motor development problems and autism will be more strongly established. Are we, on the other hand, giving parents false hope about the value of early intervention? All the evidence indicates that the earlier the intervention, the more effective it is. On the subject of false hope, we believe that hope is never false.

We understand that, like any new approach, our work will not be free of controversy. In fact, we look forward to the debate. We hope that our research and the discussions it sparks lead the way to other breakthroughs and discoveries. Now that the door is open, we want to hear from you as we work together toward a brighter future for your child. We ask that you share your experiences by filling out the form on page 145 and mailing it to the address provided.

Glossary of Terms

All words that appear in *italic type* are defined within the glossary.

ABA. See *Applied Behavior Analysis*.

AIT. See *auditory integration training*.

allied reflexes. *Reflexes* that work together to achieve a certain goal, like the allied rooting and sucking reflexes that combine to enable an infant to obtain nourishment.

Applied Behavior Analysis (ABA). A method of positive reinforcement used to shape appropriate behavior and promote learning in people with *autism* and other developmental disorders.

ASD. See *Autism Spectrum Disorders*.

Asperger's syndrome. A form of *autism* typified by a higher IQ and normal language development. People with Asperger's syndrome appear to have a decreased ability to recognize and appropriately respond to social cues, and may have a specialized area of interest that they talk about obsessively.

assistive technology. Any equipment or item, whether low-tech or high-tech, that can help a disabled person function better. This technology may include picture cards that promote nonverbal communication, computers controlled by a special touch screen, and a range of other devices.

Asymmetric Tonic Neck Reflex (ATNR). An infant *reflex* triggered when a baby's head turns to one side or the other while he is lying on his back. In response, the arm and leg on the side to which the head is turning extend or straighten, while the opposite limbs bend in a pose that has been compared to that of a fencer. This is also called the fencer response.

asymmetrical crawling. A form of atypical crawling in which the actions of one side of the body do not mirror those of the other side, giving the baby's crawling a lopsided quality.

asymmetry. The condition in which one side of the body shows postures or movements that are significantly different from those of the other side. See also *persistent asymmetry.*

ATNR. See *Asymmetric Tonic Neck Reflex.*

auditory integration training (AIT). A listening therapy, created by Guy Berard, that treats people with *autism* through specially designed musical programs. AIT seeks to "retrain" the ear to hear in a more balanced way.

autism. A condition that can appear at birth or in early childhood and is characterized by movement disorders; problems with social interaction, language, nonverbal communication, and learning; repetitive behavior; and the desire for routine. In some cases, remarkable mental abilities can also appear.

Autism Spectrum Disorders (ASD). An umbrella term that includes a number of conditions, including *autism, Asperger's syndrome, Childhood Disintegrative Disorder, Rett syndrome,* and *Pervasive Developmental Disorder—Not Otherwise Specified.*

Babinski reflex. An infant *reflex* triggered when a finger or other object strokes the sole of a baby's foot upwards from the heel, across the ball of the foot. In response, the infant hyperextends his toes, fanning them out.

bilateral symmetry. Being composed of two mirror-image halves.

blink reflex. An infant *reflex* triggered when a bright light is shone into a baby's eyes. In response, the infant closes his eyes. This reflex should persist throughout life.

brain stem. The lowest extension of the brain that is responsible for those involuntary neurological functions necessary for survival, such as breathing, heartbeat, and blood pressure. The brain stem forms a bridge between the *cerebrum* and the *spinal cord.*

bridge righting. A form of atypical *righting* in which the baby, lying on his back, arches his back upwards, maintaining contact with the ground only with his heels and head. He then turns as a single unit onto his stomach.

cat-sit position. An infant position in which the baby's legs are flexed (folded) under him; his arms are straight with his hands planted on the floor, supporting his chest; and his neck is extended, lifting his head forward in a vertical position.

central nervous system. The portion of the *nervous system* composed of the brain and *spinal cord.*

cerebellum. The portion of the brain that uses feedback from the senses to fine-tune motor activity.

cerebrum. The largest and most developmentally advanced portion of the brain, responsible for all voluntary movement. The cerebrum is composed of the *frontal lobe, occipital lobe, parietal lobe,* and *temporal lobe.*

Childhood Disintegrative Disorder. A rare disorder in which a child develops normally until the age of eighteen to twenty-four months, and then has a severe loss of social and communication skills.

contralateral crawling. The typical form of crawling that usually occurs at six to eight months of age. The infant supports himself on knees and hands, with his stomach off the ground, and moves by first "stepping" one arm forward, and then stepping forward the opposite knee. This same pattern is then repeated with the second arm and knee. This form of movement, which is true crawling, is sometimes referred to as cross-crawling.

corpus callosum. The thick bridge of nerve fibers that allows the hemispheres of the brain to work together.

crawling. See *contralateral crawling; fall-over crawling; inchworm crawling; sit crawling.*

creeping. A type of infant locomotion, sometimes used before *contralateral crawling* develops, in which the infant's stomach touches the floor as he pulls himself along with his arms, dragging his legs behind him.

cross-crawling. See *contralateral crawling.*

developmental behavioral pediatrician. A doctor who is trained in the assessment and treatment of children with developmental delays, developmental disabilities, and chronic conditions that affect a child's learning or behavior.

early intervention. The provision of services for children school age or younger who are found to have a disabling condition.

echolalia. The immediate and involuntary repetition of a word or phrase spoken by another person.

endolymph. The fluid that fills the *semicircular canals* of the *vestibular system,* helping the body detect motion.

Eshkol-Wachman Movement Notation (EWMN). A movement language published in 1958 by Noa Eshkol and Avraham Wachman. EWMN enables the objective analysis of movement.

facilitated communication. A technique that uses a device (such as a keyboard) and a facilitator (a communication partner) to allow a person without functional speech to communicate.

fall-over crawling. A form of atypical crawling in which a baby begins the *con-*

tralateral crawling pattern, but shifts his weight to his second arm before moving the arm to accept it, and therefore falls over.

fencer response. See *Asymmetric Tonic Neck Reflex.*

fine motor skills. See *motor skills.*

Floortime. A therapy for *autism,* developed by Stanley Greenspan, in which a child and a therapist get down on the floor and engage in imitation play intended to help the child master developmental milestones.

frontal lobe. The portion of the *cerebrum* involved in reasoning, planning, organizing, problem solving, emotional responses, expressive language, motor activity, and the inhibition of impulsive and reflexive actions.

Galant reflex. An infant *reflex* triggered when a baby is either placed on or supported under his abdomen, and then gently stroked to one side of the spinal column, from his neck to his lower back. In response, the back curves sideways, away from the stimulus.

gap of movement synergy. A time lag in synchronization of the various movements involved in an activity.

grasping reflex. An infant *reflex* triggered when a finger or other object is placed in a baby's open palm. In response, the baby grasps the object, gripping even more strongly if the object is pulled away.

gross motor skills. See *motor skills.*

hand flapping. A pattern of movement, characteristic of some autistic children, in which the child flaps his hands at shoulder height along the sides of his body as he walks.

IDEA. See *Individuals with Disabilities Education Act.*

inchworm crawling. A form of infant locomotion sometimes used before *contralateral crawling,* in which the infant lifts his stomach off the ground, as in true crawling, but pulls himself along with his arms, dragging his legs behind him.

Individuals with Disabilities Education Act (IDEA). A federal law—originally called the Education for All Handicapped Children Act—that ensures services such as *early intervention* and *special education* to children with disabilities.

infant reflexes. See *neonatal reflexes.*

Ladder of Motor Development. The process of gaining *motor independence* in the first year of life through *motor development stages,* each of which builds upon the previous one.

learned allied reflexes. Learned *reflexes* that work together to achieve a certain goal.

linear acceleration. Motion along a line, such as that which occurs when an elevator drops beneath your body.

Moebius mouth. A mouth shape that involves a very flat lower lip and a tented, almost triangular upper lip. This condition is caused by impaired cranial nerves.

Moro reflex. An infant *reflex* triggered when a baby is startled by a loud noise, or when his head falls backwards or quickly changes position. In response, the baby first symmetrically spreads his arms and legs out wide and extends his neck, and then pulls his arms back across his body in a clasping motion. This is also called the startle reflex.

motor development stage. A rung on the *Ladder of Motor Development* at which a child learns a new motor skill, such as *righting,* crawling, sitting, or walking.

motor independence. The ability to walk without assistance from others.

motor skills. Purposeful actions. Gross motor skills involve the larger movements of the arms, legs, and feet, such as those necessary for crawling, walking, and running. Fine motor skills involve smaller muscle movements, such as those necessary for writing and sewing.

movement synergy. The coordination of various motions involved in a movement pattern.

neonatal reflexes. *Reflexes* that develop during uterine life and are apparent at a baby's birth. These responses are also called primitive reflexes.

nerve cells. See *neurons.*

nervous system. The network of specialized cells that carry information to and from all parts of the body to regulate and coordinate body activity. This system includes the brain, *spinal cord,* and *peripheral nerves.*

neurologist. A doctor who specializes in medical problems associated with the nervous system—specifically, the brain and *spinal cord.*

neurons. The special cells that make up the brain, *spinal cord,* and *peripheral nerves.* Neurons are also referred to as nerve cells.

nutritional therapy. A therapy that involves dietary changes and/or the use of supplements to help relieve the symptoms of a condition.

occipital lobe. The portion of the *cerebrum* that processes visual information and helps in the recognition of shapes and colors.

occupational therapy. A form of treatment that uses real-life activities to help patients overcome or lessen physical disabilities, and develop *motor skills* that aid in daily living.

parachute reflex. An infant *reflex* that causes a child who is falling to extend his arms forward, protecting his head and chest.

parietal lobe. The portion of the *cerebrum* involved in visual attention, touch perception, the manipulation of objects, goal-directed voluntary motion, and the integration of the senses.

PDD-NOS. See *Pervasive Developmental Disorder—Not Otherwise Specified.*

peripheral nerves. The nerves that run from the *spinal cord* and *brain stem* to the other parts of the body.

persistent asymmetry. An asymmetry of movement or posture that lasts for a month or more. See also *asymmetry.*

Pervasive Developmental Disorder—Not Otherwise Specified (PDD-NOS). A condition in which the individual has many, but not all, of the symptoms of *autism,* but experiences relatively mild forms of these symptoms as compared with those of an autistic individual.

physical therapy. A form of treatment that uses manipulation, exercise, cold, heat, and other physical agents to facilitate normal physical function.

post-rotatory nystagmus. An involuntary eye movement triggered when an individual is spun around. The eyes repeatedly first move slowly across the range of motion, and then reset quickly to the starting position.

primitive reflexes. See *neonatal reflexes.*

primitive walk. A walking pattern that is appropriate for a young infant, but is seen in an older child who should be using a more mature walking pattern.

proprioceptive system. A system of feedback consisting of nerves that monitor internal changes in the body brought about by movement. This system conveys information that is used by the body to coordinate motor activity.

RDI. See *Relationship Development Intervention.*

reflex. A fixed movement pattern that occurs automatically in response to a specific stimulus.

reflex of approach. A *reflex* that causes an individual to increase contact with a stimulus. One example is the *grasping reflex,* which causes a baby to grip an object that is placed in his open palm.

reflex of avoidance. A *reflex* that causes an individual to decrease contact with a stimulus. One example is the blink reflex, which causes an infant to close his eyes when a bright light is shone into them.

refrigerator mother. A slang term, coined by Leo Kanner and popularized by Bruno Bettelheim, once used to describe the mothers of autistic children. The theory that a child's *autism* is caused by a mother's lack of emotional warmth has since been discredited.

Relationship Development Intervention (RDI). A type of therapy—combining elements of *Applied Behavior Analysis, Floortime,* and other treatments—designed to help children with *autism.*

Rett syndrome. A disorder in which a child at first develops normally, but then begins to experience a loss of purposeful use of the hands, distinctive hand movements, slowed brain and head growth, loss of speech, and the inability to perform motor functions.

righting. The process through which an infant independently turns over from lying on his back to lying on his stomach.

rooting reflex. An infant *reflex* triggered when the area around the mouth is touched. In response, the baby turns his head towards the stimulus, opens his mouth, and searches (roots) for the stimulus.

rump-up crawling. A form of atypical crawling in which the baby leans forward on his arms as if to crawl, but instead of stepping forward with his hands and knees, gets "stuck" with his rump (buttocks) raised in the air and his head on the floor.

saccule. A membranous sac, located in the *vestibular system,* that detects up-and-down motion.

semicircular canals. Structures in the inner ear that are designed to detect motion on a single plane.

sensory integration therapy. A form of treatment, developed originally by Jean Ayres, that teaches the nervous system to properly interpret sensory input and respond in an appropriate manner. Usually performed by a physical or occupational therapist, this therapy is designed to improve concentration, physical balance, *motor skills,* and impulse control.

sit crawling. A form of atypical crawling in which the baby assumes a knees-out sitting position, and then tries to pull himself forward with his arms while his legs remain folded under him.

special education. Teaching that is modified for students with special needs such as physical or developmental disabilities.

speech and language therapy. A form of therapy used to improve verbal skills and, in some cases, to enhance nonverbal communication and social skills as well.

spinal cord. The thick cord of tissue that extends from the brain through the vertebrae of the spinal column, carrying signals back and forth between body and brain.

startle reflex. See *Moro reflex*.

stepping reflex. An infant *reflex* triggered by holding a baby under his arms, and allowing his feet to touch a flat surface. In response, the baby moves his feet as if to walk.

stimming. Shorthand for "self-stimulation." This term is used to describe a repetitive movement that self-stimulates one or more of the senses. Types of stimming used by autistic children can include *hand flapping*, body spinning, body rocking, the spinning of toys or other objects, and a variety of other repetitive activities.

STNR. See *symmetric tonic neck reflex*.

sucking reflex. An infant *reflex* triggered when a finger or nipple is placed in the baby's mouth. In response, the baby sucks forcefully and rhythmically on the finger or nipple, and swallows in coordination with his sucking.

swing therapy. Use of a playground swing to mature a child's *vestibular system* and thereby improve his balance and other aspects of motor and cognitive behavior.

symmetric tonic neck reflex (STNR). An infant *reflex* triggered by either extension (stretching) or flexion (bending) of the infant's head. When the head is extended backwards, it results in straightening of the arms and bending of the legs. When the head is bent forward, it causes bending of the arms and straightening of the legs.

symmetry. When describing motor skills, the condition of the two sides of the body being equally active and developed, and mirroring each other's movement patterns. See also *bilateral symmetry*.

synapse. The junction between *neurons* where a nerve impulse is transmitted from one neuron to another.

tactile system. A system of feedback, consisting of nerves under the skin, that provides the brain with information about light touch, pressure, temperature, and pain. In its most basic form, this system enables a sense of contact with the ground.

Teitelbaum Tilt Test. A technique that helps determine if a child is autistic by tilting his body at a 45-degree angle, and observing whether his head remains vertical or tilts along with his body. A nonautistic child's head will remain vertical for at least a few seconds even when his body is tilted.

temporal lobe. The portion of the *cerebrum* responsible for processing auditory information.

thimerosal. A mercury-based preservative once used routinely in vaccines given to babies. Although many people have blamed the development of autism on the use of thimerosal, it is no longer included in infant vaccines.

toe walking. An atypical form of walking, characteristic of some autistic children, in which the child walks high on the balls of his feet.

Tomatis Method. Developed by French physician Alfred A. Tomatis, a treatment that uses specialized auditory stimuli of different frequencies to improve language skills, decrease hypersensitivity to sound, enhance social skills, and otherwise lessen the symptoms of autism.

tripoding. An infant position in which the child steadies himself while seated on the floor by planting his hands on the floor in front of him. This enables the baby to sit up before he acquires the balance needed to do so unaided by his hands or other people.

uninhibited reflex. A *reflex* that is supposed to fade at a certain time in an infant's development, but fails to disappear, and thereby affects the child's acquisition of motor skills.

U-righting. A form of atypical *righting* in which the infant is able to fall onto his side, but then can go no further. To finish the turn, he raises his legs and head off the floor, creating a U-shape from which he falls onto his stomach.

utricle. A membranous sac, located in the *vestibular system,* that detects sideways motion.

vestibular system. A sensory feedback system, located in the inner ear, that detects movement and changes in the position of the head. As the body moves, this system allows it to maintain balance, position, and vertical orientation in space.

*R*esources

Throughout this book, you have learned about organizations, programs, and therapies that can provide additional information about autism and its treatments, offer emotional and practical support, or directly help your child. The listings below will enable you to make contact with the resources mentioned within the book, as well as other helpful websites and groups. Please use this list as a starting point. New information, organizations, and/or therapies are sure to arise as parents and professionals work together for the benefit of autistic children everywhere.

GENERAL INFORMATION AND SUPPORT

Autism Research Institute

Website: www.autism.com

A nonprofit organization established in 1967, the Autism Research Institute (ARI) is devoted to researching and sharing information on autism triggers, diagnosis, and treatment. The ARI data bank contains 40,000 detailed case histories of autistic children.

Autism Society of America

7910 Woodmont Avenue, Suite 300
Bethesda, MD 20814
Phone: 301-657-0881
Website: www.autism-society.org

Founded in 1965, the Autism Society of America (ASA) is the oldest and largest grassroots organization in the autism community. Visit the ASA website to learn more about autism and to access Autism Source, an online directory of ASA chapters, professionals, government resources, diagnostic centers, and service providers.

Autism Speaks
2 Park Avenue, 11th Floor
New York, NY 10016
Phone: 212-252-8584
Website: www.autismspeaks.org

Founded in 2005, Autism Speaks is dedicated to funding biomedical research into the causes, prevention, treatment, and cure for autism. The group also seeks to raise public awareness of autism, and to bring the autistic community together. The Autism Speaks website provides extensive information on autism as well as links to valuable resources. Its Video Glossary, which includes over a hundred video clips, is designed to highlight the differences between typical and delayed development so that autism can be identified as early in a child's life as possible.

First Signs, Inc.
PO Box 358
Merimac, MA 01860
Phone: 978-346-4380
Website: www.first signs.org

A national nonprofit organization founded in 1998, First Signs is dedicated to educating parents and pediatric professionals about the early warning signs of autism. The First Signs website provides information on diagnosis and treatment, early intervention, specialists, and more, as well as links to a range of resources.

Helpguide
Website: www.helpguide.org

Created in 1999, Helpguide offers over 170 noncommercial articles for people in need. Click on "Autism" for information on signs and symptoms, diagnosis, and the Autism Spectrum, as well as tips on choosing treatments and finding support.

The National Institute of Mental Health
Science Writing, Press, and Dissemination Branch
6001 Executive Boulevard, Room 8184, MSC 9663
Bethesda, MD 20892
Phone: 866-615-6464
Website: www.nimh.nih.gov

The National Institute of Mental Health (NIMH) is the largest scientific organization in the world dedicated to the understanding, treatment, and prevention of mental disorders. The NIMH website offers extensive information on autism signs and symptoms, treatments, and services.

The National Respite Locator Service

Website: www.respitelocator.org

Provided by the ARCH National Respite Network, the Respite Locator was designed to help parents and other caregivers find respite services—temporary care for their child—in their area.

PROGRAMS AND THERAPIES

Applied Behavior Analysis

The Cambridge Center for Behavioral Studies
336 Baker Avenue
Concord, MA 01742
Phone: 978-369-2227
Website: www.cambridge.org

A charitable nonprofit organization, the Cambridge Center for Behaviorial Studies (CCBS) was created to advance the understanding of behavior and its humane application to practical problems. The CCBS website provides information on both the causes of autism and the treatment of autism through the use of Applied Behavior Analysis.

Camp

Kris' Camp
3359 Creek Road
Salt Lake City, UT 84121
Phone: 801-733-0721
Website: www.kriscamp.org

Through camps in Arizona, California, and Connecticut, Kris' Camp offers a week-long program for children with autism and autism-like challenges. Physical, speech, occupational, art, and music therapists provide a multidisciplinary approach, with programs tailored to individual needs. Visit the website for answers to frequently asked questions, registration forms, and other helpful information.

Community Programs

Easter Seals
230 West Monroe Street, Suite 1800
Chicago, IL 60606
Phone: 800-221-6827
Website: www.easterseals.com

Founded in 1919, Easter Seals offers help for children and adults living with autism and other disabilities. Services include special early intervention therapies for autistic children, as well as Child Development Centers that provide child care. To find services in your area, visit the Easter Seals website and click on "Find Easter Seals Near You."

Facilitated Communication

Facilitated Communication Institute
School of Education
Syracuse University
370 Huntington Hall
Syracuse, NY 13244
Phone: 315-443-9657
Website: http://thefci.syr.edu/Index.html

Facilitated communication is a means by which a person without functional speech can communicate through the use of a keyboard or other device, and the support of a facilitator. The Facilitated Communication Institute offers training for facilitators, and through its website, provides links to important organizations and educational materials.

Floortime

The Floortime Foundation
4938 Hampden Lane, Suite 229
Bethesda, MD 20814
Website: www.floortime.org

Floortime is a form of therapeutic play in which an adult joins a child in an activity that is of interest to the child, and then builds communication and other skills during the shared activity. The Floortime Foundation's website provides information on this popular therapy, as well as a database that guides you to local Floortime clinicians.

Government Programs

The National Early Childhood Technical Assistance Center
Campus Box 8040, UNC-CH
Chapel Hill, NC 27599-8040
Phone: 919-962-2001
Website: www.nectac.org

NECTAC supports the implementation of the early childhood division of the Individuals with Disabilities Education Act (IDEA). Visit the website and click on "Map Finder" to locate programs in your state.

Listening and Music Therapy Programs

Auditory Integration Training
Berard AIT Website
Website: www.berardaitwebsite.com

Developed by Guy Berard, a French doctor, auditory integration training (AIT) was designed to help people with autism and other behavioral and learning disorders. AIT specifically addresses hearing-related problems through the use of musical programs that are modified by filtering certain frequencies of sound. Visit the website to learn more about AIT, which is provided in a center-based program.

Integrated Listening Systems
5655 S. Yosemite Street, Suite 303
Greenwood Village, CO 80111
Phone: 303-741-4544
Website: www.integratedlistening.com

Integrated Listening Systems (ILS) produces listening-therapy equipment based on the Tomatis Method. Although ILS does not provide therapy directly to children with autism, its website offers a list of trained ILS practitioners, as well as extensive information on the therapy.

Neurologic Music Therapy Services
of Arizona
2702 North 3rd Street, Suite 1000
Phoenix, AZ 85004
Phone: 602-840-6410
Website: www.nmtsa.org

The Neurologic Music Therapy Services of Arizona (NMTSA) provides rehabilitative music therapy for people with autism and other developmental disabilities by involving them in music-making. Parents can take their children to programs at NMTSA, or can learn how to work with their children at home.

The Spectrum Center
307 East 53rd Street
New York, NY 10022
Phone: 877-4AUTKID
Website: www.spectrumcentermethod.com

With its main treatment center in New York, the Spectrum Center offers on-site Tomatis Method-based listening training in combination with sensory integration techniques. Equipment is available for out-of-state families who want to provide treatment at home.

Nutritional Therapy

Autism Network for Dietary Intervention
Website: www.autismndi.com

Many parents believe that dietary changes can lessen or eliminate autism-related problems. The Autism Network for Dietary Intervention (ANDI) helps families select and maintain an appropriate diet. Visit the ANDI website for a list of practitioners, journal articles on nutrition and autism, answers to common questions, a parent support system, and more.

Parent-Training Programs

The Institutes for the Achievement of Human Potential
8801 Stenton Avenue
Wyndmoor, PA 19038
Phone: (215) 233-2050
Website: www.iahp.org

With over fifty years of experience in working with brain-damaged children, The Institutes works with parents to provide them with the knowledge they need to help their child towards wellness. A variety of courses and books are available, including a program that's individualized for each child.

Son-Rise Program
Autism Treatment Center of America
2080 S. Undermountain Road
Sheffield, MA 01257
Phone: 413-229-2100
Website: www.autistictreatmentcenter.org

Founded by Barry and Samahria Kaufman, who successfully helped their own autistic son to full recovery, the Son-Rise Program of the Autism Treatment Center teaches parents how to play with their child in a way that promotes emotional growth, socialization, and skill acquisition. The Start-Up Program offers five days of parent training. Other programs are also available.

Physical Therapy

American Physical Therapy Association
1111 North Fairfax Street
Alexandria, VA 22314-1488
Phone: 800-999-2782
Website: www.apta.org

Physical therapists (PTs) can help an autistic child learn both basic and more advanced motor skills, from standing and walking, to throwing and catching a ball. PTs can also help improve general posture, balance, coordination, and strength. Visit the website of the American Physical Therapy Association (APTA) and click on "Find a PT" for an up-to-date database of member physical therapists.

Relationship Development Intervention

Connections Center
4120 Bellaire Boulevard
Houston, TX 77025
Phone: 866-378-6405
Website: www.rdiconnect.com

Created by Dr. Steven Gutstein, Relationship Development Intervention (RDI) combines several different types of treatment, including Applied Behavior Analysis, Floortime, and sensory integration therapy. Parents receive training that allows them to use an at-home program tailored for their child. The RDI website explains the program, answers frequently asked questions, provides a message board for parents, and more.

Speech and Language Therapy

American Speech-Language-Hearing Association (ASHA)
10801 Rockville Pike
Rockville, MD 20852
Phone: 800-638-8255
Website: www.asha.org

Speech and language therapists can improve a child's verbal and nonverbal communication skills, and can even enhance social skills. Visit the website of the American Speech-Language-Hearing Association (ASHA) to learn about speech development and problems. To locate a qualified audiologist or speech-language pathologist in your area, click on "Find a Professional."

Swim Therapy

SwimAmerica
Phone: 800-356-2722
Website: www.swimamerica.org

SwimAmerica operates hundreds of professional learn-to-swim programs across America, including programs designed for infants as young as six to nine months of age. Visit the website and click on "SwimAmerica Locations" to see if lessons are offered in your area.

YMCA of the USA
101 North Wacker Drive
Chicago, IL 60606
Phone: 800-872-9622
Website: www.ymca.net

The YMCA, or Y, is a worldwide nonsectarian group. Most Ys have swimming pools and offer lessons for all age groups, including children eighteen months of age and younger. To locate a Y in your area, visit the organization's website and click on "Find Your YMCA."

Suggested Reading List

The following books and articles can help expand your knowledge of autism and its treatment. Most of the books we've included are suitable for both parents and autism professionals, and some are particularly helpful for parents who want a simple but instructive guide to the brain and the nervous system. The articles listed at the end of this section are more technical in nature. While many parents will find them interesting and informative, be aware that they were written for professionals.

BOOKS

Asimov, Isaac. *How Did We Find Out About the Brain?* New York: Walker and Company, 1987.

Although written for children, this book is a great resource for adults who want a simple explanation of the workings of the brain and the nervous system.

Doman, Glenn. *What to Do About Your Brain-Injured Child.* Garden City Park, NY: Square One Publishers, 2005.

Written by the founder of the Institutes for the Achievement of Human Potential, this guide for parents offers an at-home program designed to treat children with autism and other neurological disorders.

Doman, Glenn and Janet Doman. *How Smart Is Your Baby?* Garden City Park, NY: Square One Publishers, 2006.

How Smart Is Your Baby? details a home-based program through which parents can help their infants achieve their fullest potential.

Goddard, Sally. *A Teacher's Window Into the Child's Mind.* Eugene, OR: Fern Ridge Press, 1996.

Written by a researcher at the Institute of Neuro-Physiological Psychology in Chester, England, *A Teacher's Window* explains how a child's primitive reflexes, when gone astray, can affect his later motor and cognitive development. Effective teaching methods are offered.

Grandin, Temple. *Emergence: Labeled Autistic.* Clayton, Victoria, Australia: Warner Books, 1996.

This is Temple Grandin's inspiring account of how she learned to cope with autism. Included are her own unique perspectives on the disorder.

Grandin, Temple. *Thinking in Pictures: And Other Reports From My Life With Autism.* New York: Vintage Books, 1994.

This riveting book illustrates Grandin's autistic mind, explaining how it works in pictures rather than words, and how it enabled her to become a worldwide authority on cattle enclosure design.

Iversen, Portia. *Strange Son.* New York: Riverhead Books, 2006.

Strange Son tracks Iversen's journey to understand and find treatment for her son, Dov, who was diagnosed with autism at age two. Included is her work with Soma, a mother in India who developed a unique method of communicating with her own autistic son, who, like Dov, had no language.

Jepson, Bryan. *Changing the Course of Autism.* Boulder, CO: Sentient Publications, 2007.

Changing the Course of Autism provides an up-to-date discussion of possible causes of the disorder, with special emphasis on the physiological systems involved.

Kalina, Sigmund. *Your Nerves and Their Messages.* New York: William Morrow, 1973.

Although intended for children, this is an excellent book for any adult who wants an easy-to-understand explanation of the nervous system.

Kaufman, Barry Neil. *Son Rise: The Miracle Continues.* Tiburon, CA: HJ Kramer, 1995.

An update of the 1976 book *Son Rise, The Miracle Continues* tells the remarkable story of Barry and Samahria Kaufman, who—moving against the currents of the time— developed a way to enter their son's world and bring him out of autism. This became the basis of their Son-Rise Program.

O'Dell, Nancy E. and Patricia Cook. *Stopping ADHD.* New York: Avery, 2004.

This book looks at the underlying causes of ADD/ADHD, explaining how the reflex involved in crawling, when gone astray, affects later motor and cognitive development. Included in the book is the authors' revolutionary crawling exercise program, which can help a child focus and function normally.

Prince-Hughes, Dawn. *Songs of the Gorilla Nation: My Journey Through Autism.* New York: Harmony Books, 2004.

Prince-Hughes' memoir first explores her devastating early life experiences resulting from undiagnosed Asperger's syndrome. It then shows how contact with animals—in her case, gorillas—can have a healing effect.

Sollier, Pierre. *Listening for Wellness: An Introduction to the Tomatis Method.* The Mozart Center Press, 2005.

Easy to read for parents and teachers alike, *Listening for Wellness* reveals the basis of the Tomatis Method of listening therapy, and explains how to evaluate children and design appropriate treatment plans.

Tubbs, Janet. *Creative Therapy for Children with Autism, ADD, and Asperger's.* Garden City Park, NY: Square One Publishers, 2008.

The result of decades of working with children with behavioral problems, *Creative Therapy* presents exercises and activities designed to reduce hyperactivity, increase focus, and otherwise help the child with autism and related disorders.

JOURNAL ARTICLES

Teitelbaum, Osnat, et al. "Eshkol-Wachman Movement Notation in Diagnosis: The Early Detection of Asperger's Syndrome." *Proceedings of the National Academy of Sciences of the United States* (August 2004): vol. 101, 11909–11914. www.pubmedcentral.nih.gov/articlerender.fcgi?artid=511073

This article presents evidence that abnormal movement patterns found in infancy make possible an early diagnosis of Asperger's syndrome.

Teitelbaum, Philip, et al. "Movement Analysis in Infancy May Be Useful for Early Diagnosis of Autism." *Proceedings of the National Academy of Sciences of the United States* (November 1998): vol. 95, 13982–13987. www.pnas.org/cgi/content/full/95/23/3982

This article describes our initial study and details our findings on the link between early motor skill problems and the development of autism.

References

AUTISM

Aitken, K. "Diagnostic Issues in Autism—Are We Measuring the Emperor for Another Suit of Clothes?" *Developmental Medicine and Child Neurology* (1991): Vol. 33, 1015–1020.

Asperger, H. "Autistic Psychopathy in Childhood." In *Autism and Asperger Syndrome,* edited by Uta Frith. Cambridge, England: Cambridge University Press, 1991.

Centers for Disease Control and Prevention. "Prevalence of Autism Spectrum Disorders." *Morbidity and Mortality Weekly Report* (February 9, 2007): 56 (SS01), 12–28.

Damasio, AR and RG Maurer. "A Neurological Model for Childhood Autism." *Archives of Neurology* (1978): Vol. 35, 777–786.

Diagnostic and Statistical Manual of Mental Disorders, Fourth Edition. Arlington, VA: American Psychiatric Publishing, 2000.

Filipek, PA, et al. "The Screening and Diagnosis of Autistic Spectrum Disorders." *Journal of Autism and Developmental Disorders* (1999): Vol. 29, 439–484.

Gillberg, C and I Winnergard. "Childhood Psychosis in a Case of Moebius Syndrome." *Neuropediatrics* (1984): Vol. 15, 147–149.

Goldblatt, D and D Williams. " 'I an Sniling!' Moebius' Syndrome Inside and Out." *Journal of Child Neurology* (1986): Vol. 1, 71–78.

Jepson, Bryan. *Changing the Course of Autism.* Boulder, CO: Sentient Publications, 2007.

Kanner, Leo. "Autistic Disturbances of Affective Contact." *Nervous Child* 2 (1943): 217–250.

Miller, MT, et al. "The Puzzle of Autism: An Ophthalmologic Contribution." *Transactions of the American Ophthalmological Society* (1998): Vol. XCVI, 369–387.

Purdon Martin, J, et al. "The Negative Symptoms of Basal Gangliar Disease." *Lancet* (July 14, 1962): 62–66.

AUTISM TREATMENTS

Lovaas, OI. "Behavioral Treatment and Normal Educational and Intellectual Functioning in Young Autistic Children." *Journal of Consulting and Clinical Psychology* (1987): Vol. 55, 3–9.

"New Study Shows Autism-Related Developmental 'Red Flags' Identifiable at Age Two in Children with Autism Spectrum Disorders." www.blackwellpublishing.com

CHILD REFLEXES

Fiorentino, Mary R. *Normal and Abnormal Development: The Influence of Primitive Reflexes on Motor Development.* Springfield, IL: Charles C. Thomas, 1976.

Goddard, Sally. *A Teacher's Window Into the Child's Mind.* Eugene, OR: Fern Ridge Press, 1996.

O'Dell, Nancy E. and Patricia Cook. *Stopping ADHD.* New York: Avery, 2004.

Paine, RS, et al. "Evolution of Postural Reflexes in Normal Infants and in the Presence of Chronic Brain Syndromes." *Neurology* (1964): Vol. 14, 1036–1048.

Peiper, Albrecht. *Cerebral Function in Infancy and Childhood.* New York: Consultants Bureau, 1963.

INFANT AND CHILD DEVELOPMENT

Ayres, A. Jean. *Sensory Integration and Learning Disorders.* Los Angeles: Western Psychological Services, 1973.

Cermak, SA; EJ Quintero; and PM Cohen. "Developmental Age Trends in Crossing the Body Midline in Normal Children." *The American Journal of Occupational Therapy* (May 1980): Vol. 34, 313-319.

Doman, Glenn. *What to Do About Your Brain-Injured Child.* Garden City Park, NY: Square One Publishers, 2005.

Doman, Glenn and Janet Doman. *How Smart Is Your Baby?* Garden City Park, NY: Square One Publishers, 2006.

McGraw, Myrtle, B. *The Neuromuscular Maturation of the Human Infant.* Cambridge, England: Cambridge University Press, 1991.

MOVEMENT NOTATION AND ANALYSIS

Eshkol, Noa and Abraham Wachman. *Movement Notation.* London: Weidenfeld and Nicolson, 1958.

Eshkol, Noa and John Harries. *EWMN, Part I.* Holon, Israel: The Movement Notation Society, 2001.

Eshkol, Noa and John Harries. *EWMN, Part II.* Holon, Israel: The Movement Notation Society, 2004.

Fay, T. "The Origin of Human Movement." *American Journal of Psychiatry* (1955): Vol. 111, 644–652.

*O*bservation Journal

Throughout this book, we have emphasized the importance of recording your infant's motor development either on paper or in the form of a videotape. If you have chosen to record some or all of your child's progress on paper, this Observation Journal will come in handy. For each month of your child's first year, you'll find space in which to note his progress up the Ladder of Motor Development. As you use this journal, remember that while it's important to note milestones such as righting, crawling, sitting, and walking, it's equally important to describe *how* your child is achieving these milestones. If he's righting himself, is he doing so in the typical manner discussed on pages 51 to 52, or is he using an atypical form that may indicate a problem? Similarly, you'll want to note how he is crawling, sitting, and walking. Always be sure to observe if his movements are symmetrical or asymmetrical, and to make notations about his reflexes as well.

When observing your baby, be aware that infants are not on strict timetables regarding their motor development. Some children begin to walk earlier than others, for instance, and walking earlier is no better than walking a little later. What matters most is how your child walks. Also keep in mind that many children briefly show an atypical form of movement when they are struggling to master a motor skill. They may learn to crawl backwards before they begin to crawl forwards. They may at first move their arms asymmetrically when walking, and master the proper arm movements only after further practice. You should be concerned only if the unusual motion becomes persistent by lasting for a month or more.

MONTH 1

Observations

MONTH 2

Observations

MONTH 3

Observations

_____

_____

_____

_____

_____

_____

_____

_____

_____

_____

_____

_____

_____

_____

_____

_____

_____

_____

_____

_____

_____

MONTH 4

Observations

MONTH 5

Observations

MONTH 6

Observations

MONTH 7

Observations

_____

_____

_____

_____

_____

_____

_____

_____

_____

_____

_____

_____

_____

_____

_____

_____

_____

_____

_____

_____

MONTH 8

Observations

MONTH 9

Observations

_____

_____

_____

_____

_____

_____

_____

_____

_____

_____

_____

_____

_____

_____

_____

_____

_____

_____

_____

_____

MONTH 10

Observations

MONTH 11

Observations

_____

_____

_____

_____

_____

_____

_____

_____

_____

_____

_____

_____

_____

_____

_____

_____

_____

_____

_____

_____

_____

_____

_____

_____

MONTH 12

Observations

_____
_____
_____
_____
_____
_____
_____
_____
_____
_____
_____
_____
_____
_____
_____
_____
_____
_____
_____
_____
_____
_____
_____
_____

*P*arent Questionnaire

We would like to know whether the information in this book has proven useful to you. The answers you provide will serve to guide us in helping other parents. Please respond to the questions below either by filling out the form on our website (www.doesyourbabyhaveautism.com), or by completing the form below and mailing it to:

Department AR
Square One Publishers
115 Herricks Road
Garden City Park, NY 11040

1. What is the age and gender of your child? _____   _____

2. Did you notice any of the movement disturbances described in this book in your baby, and at what age?

_____

_____

_____

_____

_____

3. Did you perform the Tilt Test on your baby? If so, what was the result?

_____

_____

_____

_____

4. After noticing that "something was wrong," what did you do to help your baby? Did you, for instance, take him to your pediatrician, enroll him in a program, etc?

_____

_____

_____

_____

_____

_____

5. So far, what has been the result of your efforts to help your child? Have you, for instance, noticed an improvement in your child's motor skills?

_____

_____

_____

_____

_____

_____

_____

_____

_____

_____

Optional Information

In the future, we may wish to contact you to learn more about your child's progress. If desired, please provide the following contact information:

Name_____

Address_____

Phone Number _____ Email Address: _____

*I*ndex

About The Authors

Osnat Teitelbaum was born and raised in Israel. She studied movement and movement notation under Professor Noa Eshkol, first at Seminar Hakibbutzim College and then at Tel Aviv University. Her work with Professor Eshkol spanned more than fifteen years. Since 1989, the author has taught movement analysis in the Psychology Department of the University of Florida. Ms. Teitelbaum has co-authored a number of ground-breaking academic articles, including "Movement Analysis in Infancy May Be Useful for Early Diagnosis of Autism," "Eshkol-Wachman Movement Notation in Diagnosis: The Early Detection of Asperger's Syndrome," and "Reflexes Gone Astray in Autism in Infancy." She and her husband, Dr. Philip Teitelbaum, lecture around the country on the detection of autism through the observation of infant motor skills.

Philip Teitelbaum, PhD, completed his doctoral degree in Physiological Psychology at Johns Hopkins University in Baltimore, Maryland. He has been a professor at Harvard University, the University of Pennsylvania, and the University of Illinois, and is presently a Graduate Research Professor at the University of Florida. A member of the National Academy of Sciences, Dr. Teitelbaum has published over one hundred articles in the field of psychology. He is also the author of *Fundamental Principles of Physiological Psychology,* and editor of *Motivation: Handbook of Behavioral Neurobiology.*

CREATIVE THERAPY

For Children with Autism, ADD, and Asperger's

Janet Tubbs

It is no easy task to find a teaching technique that can truly change the course of a child with special needs. Thirty years ago, when Janet Tubbs began working with children who had low self-esteem and behavioral problems, she developed a successful program using art, music, and movement. Believing that unconventional children required unconventional therapies, she then took her program one step further—she applied it to children with autism, ADD/ADHD, and Asperger's Syndrome. Her innovative methods and strategies not only worked, but actually defied the experts. In this new book, Janet Tubbs has put together a powerful teaching tool to help parents, therapists, and teachers work with their children.

The book is divided into two parts. Part One provides an overview of Autism Spectrum Disorders and introduces and explains Janet's novel approach to teaching. Her goal is to balance the child's body, mind, and spirit through proven techniques. Part Two provides a wide variety of exercises, activities, and games that are both fun and effective.

A child may appear stubborn and difficult, but that doesn't mean that the child isn't intelligent, curious, or creative. With the right treatment, such a child can be reached, taught, and set on the road to improvement. The lessons provided in this book may be just what you and your child have been waiting for.

$18.95 • 336 pages • 7.5 x 9-inch quality paperback • ISBN 978-0-7570-0300-4

WHAT TO DO ABOUT YOUR BRAIN-INJURED CHILD

Glenn Doman

In this updated classic, Glenn Doman—founder of The Institutes for the Achievement of Human Potential and pioneer in the treatment of the brain-injured children—brings real hope to thousands of children who have been sentenced to a life of institutional confinement.

In *What To Do About Your Brain-Injured Child,* Doman recounts the story of The Institutes' tireless effort to refine treatment of the brain injured. He shares the staff's lifesaving techniques and the tools used to measure—and ultimately improve—visual, auditory, tactile, mobile, and manual development. Doman explains the unique methods of treatment that are constantly being improved and expanded, and then describes the program with which parents can treat their own children at home in a familiar and loving environment. Included throughout are case histories, drawings, and helpful charts and diagrams.

Twenty thousand families from over one hundred nations have brought their children to The Institutes. The great majority of these children have done better than their parents had hoped, and for each of these families, this book was the starting point.

$18.95 • 336 pages • 6 x 9-inch quality paperback • ISBN 978-0-7570-0186-4

HOW TO TEACH YOUR BABY TO READ

Glenn Doman and Janet Doman

As the founder of The Institutes for the Achievement of Human Potential, Glenn Doman has demonstrated time and again that young children are far more capable of learning than we ever imagined. In *How To Teach Your Baby To Read,* he and daughter Janet show just how easy it is to teach a young child to read. They explain how to begin and expand the reading program, how to make and organize necessary materials, and how to more fully develop your child's reading potential.

By following the simple daily program presented in *How To Teach Your Baby To Read,* you will give your baby a powerful advantage that will last a lifetime.

$13.95 • 288 pages • 6 x 9-inch quality paperback • ISBN 978-0-7570-0185-7

HOW TO TEACH YOUR BABY MATH

Glenn Doman and Janet Doman

Glenn and Janet Doman have not only shown that children from birth to age six learn better and faster than older children do, but have given it practical application. *How To Teach Your Baby Math* demonstrates just how easy it is to teach a young child mathematics through the development of thinking and reasoning skills. It explains how to begin and expand the math program, how to make and organize necessary materials, and how to more fully develop your child's math potential.

By following the simple daily program in a relaxed and loving way, you will enable your child to experience the joy of learning—as have millions of children the world over.

$13.95 • 240 pages • 6 x 9-inch quality paperback • ISBN 978-0-7570-0184-0

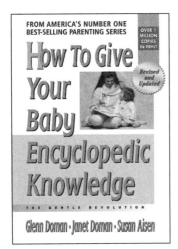

HOW TO GIVE YOUR BABY ENCYCLOPEDIC KNOWLEDGE

Glenn Doman, Janet Doman, and Susan Aisen

How To Give Your Baby Encyclopedic Knowledge shows you how simple it is to teach a young child about the arts, science, and nature. Your child will recognize the insects in the garden, learn about the countries of the world, discover the beauty of a painting by Van Gogh, and more. This book explains how to begin and develop this remarkable program, how to create and organize necessary materials, and how to more fully cultivate your child's learning ability.

Very young children not only can learn, but can learn far better and faster than older children. Let *How To Give Your Baby Encyclopedic Knowledge* be the first step in a lifetime of achievement.

$13.95 • 318 pages • 6 x 9-inch quality paperback • ISBN 978-0-7570-0182-6

HOW TO MULTIPLY YOUR BABY'S INTELLIGENCE

Glenn Doman and Janet Doman

Too often, we waste our children's most important years by refusing to allow them to learn everything they can at a time when it is easiest for them to absorb new information. *How To Multiply Your Baby's Intelligence* provides a comprehensive program that shows you just how easy and pleasurable it is to teach your young child how to read, to understand mathematics, and to literally multiply his or her overall learning potential. It explains how to begin and expand a remarkable proven program, how to make and organize the necessary materials, and how to more fully develop your child's learning ability, preparing him or her for a lifetime of success.

$15.95 • 400 pages • 6 x 9-inch quality paperback • ISBN 978-0-7570-0183-3

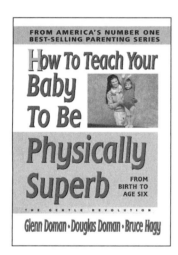

HOW TO TEACH YOUR BABY TO BE PHYSICALLY SUPERB

Glenn Doman, Douglas Doman, and Bruce Hagy

The early development of mobility in newborns is a vital part of their future ability to learn and grow to full potential. In *How to Teach Your Baby To Be Physically Superb,* Glenn Doman—founder of The Institutes for the Achievement of Human Potential—along with Douglas Doman and Bruce Hagy guide you in maximizing your child's physical capabilities. The authors first discuss each stage of mobility, and then explain how you can create an environment that will help your baby more easily reach that stage. Full-color charts, photographs, illustrations, and detailed yet easy-to-follow instructions are included to help you establish and use an effective home program that guides your baby from birth to age six.

$29.95 • 296 pages • 7.5 x 10.5-inch hardback • ISBN 978-0-7570-0192-5

HOW TO TEACH YOUR BABY TO SWIM

Douglas Doman

Teaching an infant or toddler to swim is not only a matter of safety, but also a great way to stimulate the child's physical coordination, concentration, and intelligence. That's right. By teaching your baby the proper swimming techniques, you can actually enhance his or her learning ability. You will also make your child happier, healthier, and more self-confident. Based on the revolutionary learning principles developed at The Institutes for the Achievement of Human Potential, *How To Teach Your Baby To Swim* is a clear and easy-to-follow guide to teaching your child swimming basics.

$14.95 • 128 pages • 7.5 x 9-inch quality paperback • ISBN 978-0-7570-0198-7

MASSAGING YOUR BABY
The Joy of Touch Time
Dr. Elaine Fogel Schneider

The power of touch is real and has been scientifically shown to have remarkable effects. For infants, it encourages relaxation; improves sleep patterns; reduces discomfort from teething, colic, and gas; strengthens digestive and circulatory systems; and does so much more. For parents, it nurtures bonding, increases communication, promotes parenting skills, and reduces stress levels. Now, massage expert Dr. Elaine Fogel Schneider has written the ultimate guide to using infant massage at home. *Massaging Your Baby* begins by explaining why massage is so beneficial. It then provides an easy-to-follow step-by-step guide to effective massage.

$15.95 • 224 pages • 7.5 x 9-inch quality paperback • ISBN 978-0-7570-0263-2

POTTY TRAINING YOUR BABY
A Practical Guide for Easier Toilet Training

Katie Warren

Contrary to traditional belief, the transition from diaper to potty can be started even before your child's first birthday—and completed by the second! Katie Warren advises taking advantage of the early months, when babies do most of their communicating on an emotional level, as children understand things intuitively much sooner than they understand words. *Potty Training Your Baby* provides information on everything from where to buy a potty to dealing with those inevitable little "accidents." Perhaps most important, the author shows you how to turn this often dreaded and frustrating task into a time of growth and learning for both you and your child.

$9.95 • 104 pages • 6 x 9-inch quality paperback • ISBN 978-0-7570-0180-2

HOW TO MAXIMIZE YOUR CHILD'S LEARNING ABILITY
A Complete Guide to Choosing and Using the Best Computer Games, Activities, Learning Aids, Toys, and Tactics for Your Child
Lauren Bradway, PhD, and Barbara Albers Hill

Over twenty years ago, Dr. Lauren Bradway discovered that all children have specific learning styles. Some learn best through visual stimulation; others, through sound and language; and others, through touch. In this book, Dr. Bradway first shows you how to determine your child's inherent style. She then aids you in carefully selecting the toys, activities, and educational strategies that will help reinforce the talents your child was born with, and encourage those skills that come less easily.

$14.95 • 288 pages • 6 x 9-inch quality paperback • ISBN 978-0-7570-0096-6